AF255470

HOW TO MANAGE A FLOURISHING CHURCH

Albrecht Dürer – The Last Supper (1523)

ADELBERT SCHOLTZ

HOW TO MANAGE A FLOURISHING CHURCH

A PRACTICAL GUIDE FOR MINISTERS, PASTORS, PRIESTS, AND ELDERS

RESOURCE *Publications* • Eugene, Oregon

CONTENTS

PREFACE

This book is the result of my experiences in the ministry of three congregations of the Nederduitse Gereformeerde Kerk (Dutch Reformed Church) in South Africa, as a part-time minister in two congregations in Europe while doing advanced study there, as a part-time lecturer in practical theology at two South African universities, as well as extensive reading and research for two doctorates and other post-graduate qualifications.

My involvement in the commissions for church polity of the General Synod and of two provincial synods of my denomination gave me valuable insight into the difficulties many congregations and their ministers faced due to a lack of management skills.

Where no authority is quoted in the footnotes to support a certain statement or idea, it may be assumed that that thought or conclusion is contained in one of my academic theses (see Bibliography), or is the result of my personal experience.

The object of this book is to help all those who are in leading positions in their churches to understand their tasks and challenges better. It is hoped that the insights and knowledge contained in this book will result in more flourishing churches, especially in our time where many churches are struggling on account of dwindling membership numbers and financial constraints.

Adelbert Scholtz, December 2022

INTRODUCTION

When I was doing research for my Ph.D. in (industrial) psychology regarding the working conditions of ministers of religion, it transpired that many ministers felt that they were not adequately trained to help with the management of their churches. Later, when I was helping with a two-year course in theology for lay people, as well as when I was lecturing part-time at the Department of Religion and Theology of the University of the Western Cape, South Africa, many of my students – who were already in the ministry – uttered the wish to receive some training in the administration and management of their churches.

It is, therefore, clear that there is need for a publication such as this. It goes without saying that the management and administration of the Church of Christ must be performed in a Christian way – that is, according to Christian principles as we find them in the Bible, the Word of God.

The temptation exists to manage the church as if it is a business concern. It must always be remembered that the church is a unique type of organization, a creation of God.

Therefore, this guide is not just another guide on how to manage an organization. We are dealing here with a unique organization, the Christian Church, which cannot be compared in all respects to other types of organizations. There are similarities, of course. Any church consists of people who have different roles to play – just as in any other organization. But the big difference is that the church is not a human creation or invention and the final authority rests with the King of the Church, Jesus Christ.

In this guide, therefore, we will investigate the biblical principles for managing and administering the church. There is much, though, that we can also learn from secular business principles, as long as they do not clash with biblical principles and lead the church away from its primary task, namely to serve the interests of the Kingdom of God.

Every chapter contains some Bible study. It is recommended that the reader answers the questions regarding the relevant biblical texts and then compare his/her answers with the rest of the relevant chapter.

This guide is aimed at all Christians who have leadership positions in their respective churches or are involved with the administration and management of their churches – pastors, priests, elders, deacons, treasurers, choir leaders, secretaries, coordinators of Sunday Schools *etcetera*. Although this book was written with a South African environment in mind it may be fruitfully applied in any other country.

This book presupposes the traditional Protestant point of view, although church leaders adhering to other brands of Christianity may, certainly, learn much from this book. Protestantism is built upon the following four principles:

- The *only* source for the contents of our faith is the Word of God in the Bible (*sola Scriptura*);
- Our salvation is *only* dependent upon the work, death and resurrection of Jesus Christ (*solus Christus*);
- We can *only* be saved through faith in Jesus Christ, not our own good works (*sola fide*); and
- Our salvation is the result of God's grace *only*, not our own contributions or merit (*sola gratia*).

Throughout this book, only the male form of the personal pronoun is used (he, his and him). This must not be construed as sexist and is only done for the sake of better readability. It is always cumbersome to write he/she, his/her or him/her. The male form, therefore, presupposes the female form.

1. THE CHURCH OF JESUS CHRIST

Read: 1 Thess 1: 1; 2 Thess 1: 1
To whom does the church belong?

The Church of Jesus Christ is described by many metaphors in the Bible. It is called the body of Christ, the temple of the Holy Spirit, the people of God, the flock of Christ or the army of Christ. All these metaphors imply that a church has to be led, organized and managed.

Most Christian churches subscribe to the Apostles' Creed, the oldest summary of the Christian faith outside of the New Testament. In this creed, the believer states,

> "I believe in... the holy Catholic Christian Church, the communion of saints,..."

If we want to discuss the administration and management of the Christian Church, it is necessary that we get a good idea of what exactly we mean by the words quoted above. The Church is a unique type of organization – it is holy, catholic and Christian. It is a community of saints. This cannot be said of any other organization on earth.

There are various types of organizations in our contemporary society. They are all the products of human ingenuity and inventiveness. Human beings decided to found these entities, but that cannot be said of the Christian Church because it is the creation of God. It has Jesus Christ as its head. It is the temple of the Holy Spirit. It finds its principles and guidelines in the holy Bible, the Word of God.

When the management and administration of the Church is being investigated, these principles may never be ignored. The Church is not an organization that may ever be structured and administered in the same way as a business entity, a government department or a sports club.

Therefore – it must be explained what is being meant when we use the word "Church" before we can discuss its management and administration.

Read: Gal 1: 11–24
How did Paul become an apostle?

The Church

In most countries there is a wide variety of churches and denominations. Although they sometimes differ regarding doctrinal issues and liturgy, they, nevertheless, are all part of the Church of the Lord.

The world-wide Christian church is an *invisible* entity. It is, nevertheless, a reality. Paul wrote in Gal 1: 13: "For you have heard of my early career in Judaism – how I furiously persecuted the Church of God, and made havoc of it." This "Church of God" is a general concept and cannot be localised in any geographical spot.

When we want to observe the *visible* church, we must visit a particular congregation on the Lord's Day when the members gather for worship. The church building is mostly clearly visible and a notice board proclaims what type of church it is and when services are being held. The activities of the church are often also visible during the week when Christians are busy with Bible study groups, with charity, when they battle against injustice and when they give witness of their faith and principles.

It happens sometimes that we also see something of the church in a wider context when the congregations of a certain denomination send delegates to a synod, general meeting, conference or council.

It is a commendable to be loyal towards the church or congregation to which we belong. We believe that God has placed us there. But we ought also to be loyal to the church in general, the Church of Jesus Christ. We are, after all, children of the same Heavenly Father.

Read: 2 Pet 1: 8–15
How are members of the church selected to become members?

Read: Rev 7: 13–17
How does one qualify to become one of the saints in heaven?

A Holy Church

One sometimes hears the complaint that certain people don't feel at home in the church, due to the many hypocrites in the church. That is not how God sees the members of the church who belong to Jesus Christ. In his eyes, they are holy people, saints (1 Cor 1: 1–2; Eph 1: 1).

We must understand this term of sainthood. When the Bible mentions "saints" it doesn't mean sinless and perfect people. Somebody can be a saint, a holy person, simply because he belongs to God. That is true of all believers. We are God's property because Christ paid for us with his life – and therefore everyone has to dedicate his whole life, including his time, belongings, talents, opportunities and energy to the service of God. Saints are, therefore, people who serve God and who are set apart from those who don't know God.

That means that the church, comprised of saints, is also a holy institution. Many people regard the church simply as a social institution – the product of people who are interested in religion and who like to get together. The church is much more than that.

The membership of the church is, in last resort, in the hands of God. It is God who calls people and equips people (2 Pet 1: 10). He grants the status of sainthood on his children because He has forgiven them their sins (Rev 7: 13–17).

Nobody deserves this privilege because we are all sinners. It is only through the grace of God that we can become saints, holy people. That puts the obligation on us to lead lives that demonstrate our sainthood by actively being obedient to all God's wishes for our lives, by being caring, humble and thankful. If we do that nobody can accuse us of being hypocrites.

Read: Acts 15: 12–21
Who may belong to the church?

A Catholic Church

The church of Jesus Christ is in a paradoxical state. On the one hand it is a very exclusive organization, but on the other hand it is also an organization to which any person may belong.

The church is exclusive because not anybody can belong to it. Membership is strictly controlled and restricted. Only persons, who have accepted Jesus Christ as their saviour, who have put all their trust and faith in Him, who are the property of Christ, who are children of God and who have the Holy Spirit in their lives, are welcome.

The church is, after all, the body of Christ, the flock of the Lord, the temple of the Holy Spirit, the people of God. It is, therefore, a special kind of organization that is meant for special people.

These special people cannot boast about wonderful achievements, characteristics or experiences. They are the people who have received God's grace and who see their relationship with Christ as a precious gift. But that is also the reason why the church doors are open to everyone. Any type of person may become a child of God, may receive the Holy Spirit and may accept Jesus Christ in faith.

In the time of the apostles there were those who wanted to limit membership of the church to those who have received circumcision and have, in effect, became Jewish (Acts 11 and 15). In later ages there were also those who wanted to restrict church membership to certain ethnic groups or social classes.

The Lord has called all classes of people to become members of his church right from the start. In his circle of disciples/apostles, Jesus included two men with Greek names, namely Andrew and Philip, apart from the other who had Jewish names (Acts 1: 13). These two were probably men with a Greek background

When we read the letters of the apostle Paul, the earliest Christian documents we have, we see that he regarded Jews, Greeks, Romans, people from Africa, rich people, slaves, men, women, important people and ordinary folk as his brothers and sisters in Christ.

All sorts of people are, therefore, welcome to believe in Jesus Christ and to belong to the Church of the Lord. The Church is, in other words, catholic or universal, a body that transcends all human barriers.

A Christian Church and the Communion of Saints
It sometimes happens that people of the church forget that the church is supposed to be Christian. Paul had to admonish the members of

the church of Corinth in his first letter to them to behave as Christians ought to behave. It appears that they fought amongst each other, drank too much, took part in pagan ceremonies and lived immoral lives. They forgot to be Christians who belong to Christ.

Another good example of a church that forgot to be Christian is the church of Laodicea of which we read in Rev 3. John wrote to them on behalf of Christ: "Because you are lukewarm and neither hot nor cold, before long I will vomit you out of My mouth" (Rev 3: 16). To the church in Sardis, John wrote: "I know your doings – you are supposed to be alive, but in reality, you are dead" (Rev 3: 1).

It is clear that these churches neglected to be Christian, to demonstrate the fact that they were supposed to belong to Christ. The Lord called upon them to undergo a reformation and a revival. That is a process that has to be continually pursued in the church. We must constantly measure ourselves against the standard and example that Christ set during his ministry on earth. That we are supposed to be Christian, Christ-like, must also be reflected in the way the church is being administered and managed. If we don't conform to those standards then we must initiate a process of reformation and revival.

We must ask ourselves on a daily basis: do we live as Christians? Do we care enough about our brothers and sisters in the Lord? Do we demonstrate enough charity towards those in need? Do we give enough of our time and energy to further the interests of the kingdom of God? Do we withstand all that is bad, wrong, evil and hurtful? Do we follow the example of Jesus Christ? Are the leaders in our church following the leadership style of Jesus?

Christians also believe in the communion of saints, the idea that people who belong to the Lord also belong together. That is why Christians go to church meetings on the Lord's Day and why they care for each other. Christians see each other as brothers and sisters in Christ, as co-members of the household of God. This caring for each other must also become visible in the administration and management of the church.

We may never forget that the church to which we belong is supposed to be an organization that is holy, catholic or universal, Christian and where the communion of saints is actively sought.

It has already been mentioned that here is a visible and an invisible church. The invisible church is the world-wide church to which all believers of all ages belong. The visible church is to be found wherever we see a gathering of Christians.

A distinction is often made between the triumphant church and the militant church. The triumphant church will someday exist in heaven after the second coming of Christ and Judgment Day. Then all the chosen children of God will be gathered and the church will be complete – also complete in the sense that its struggle against evil and godlessness will be something of the past. The militant church is to be seen in our day. That is the church that is still struggling against evil in all its forms and fighting, just to be able to survive in a world that is not well disposed towards the Christian Gospel.

In this book, we are concerned with the visible church and the militant church – the church as we experience it in our daily lives, here on earth. The visible church, as we see it in our own congregation, is also the militant church that is fighting as the army of Jesus Christ. This church has to have leaders, organizers, officials and administrators.

2. ADMINISTRATION AND MANAGEMENT ACCORDING TO THE BIBLE

Read: Ps 24: 1–2
Is our Christian religion only concerned with our souls and the spiritual side of life? Motivate your answer.

Read: Tit 1: 7
What is the task of an elder?

Read: Matt 20: 8; Luke 12: 42–44;16: 1–13; 1 Cor 4: 1–2
Does the church need people who are good administrators? Why?

Read: Rom 12: 5–8 (especially vs 8)
Why are the various "gifts" given to the church? Where does management come into the picture?

There can be no doubt that the church of Christ has to be managed and administered. The church is, after all, an organization comprised of a number of people who are organized into various groups: the church council, the choir, the Sunday school, youth groups, Bible study groups, care groups and so forth. No church can survive without money and the management of finances is part and parcel of the administration of every church.

The biblical passages quoted above all make it clear that there have to be leaders in every church to oversee the workings of that church, whether it is the local church or the church in a wider context. One may see the following principles of church government as essential:

Discipline

Although it is expected of Christians to be spontaneous in their love, charity, witnessing and worship, it is also necessary that the church be a disciplined community where things are done in an orderly and proper manner.

The apostle Paul reminds us:

- "God is not a God of confusion, but of peace" (1 Cor 14: 33);
- "Let all things be done decently and in order" (1 Cor 14: 40); and
- "Let all things be done to build each other up" (1 Cor 14: 26).

Openness, Accountability and Integrity

The church is not a secret society and everything done in the church must be done in such a manner that it can endure the light of day.

No decision of any ecclesiastic governing body may, of course, clash with the principles we find in the Bible. God expects of his children to act with honesty, truthfulness and integrity in all walks of life, including the governance of the church. We read in James 5: 12 – "Let your `yes' be simply `yes,' and your `no' be simply `no;' that you may not come under condemnation."

For that reason, it is imperative that the financial books of any church have to be audited annually and that members of the congregation are welcome to inspect the financial statements and records.

All the decisions of a church council ought to be communicated to the members of that congregation – apart from confidential matters where the good name and reputation of certain people have to be protected.

A Perspective on the World

No church exists for its own sake. The church, as the body of Jesus Christ, is supposed to be the eyes, ears, hands, mouth, feet and heart of Jesus Christ. Christians are called upon to continue the work that Jesus did during his ministry on earth: to bring the love of God to our neighbors, to feed the hungry, to house the homeless, to clothe the naked, to visit the sick, to console those who are weeping, to protect those who are powerless and to condemn and fight wrongdoing and injustice in all its forms.

The task of the church, therefore, is to serve God and to serve humanity. This is being done by preaching the Gospel and by reaching out to those who need help – irrespective of race, color, language, gender or social status.

Discrimination in any form may never occur in the church (James 2: 1–4). Discrimination in this sense means that certain people are treated less well than the others on account of the fact that they belong to a certain group, class, race or gender. That may never happen in the church.

Jesus preached the Kingdom of God or the Kingdom of Heaven. This Kingdom is to be found wherever people submit to the authority and kingship of God, who is master of his whole creation. When people obey God's ordinances, they are working to further the interests of the Kingdom of God. The church is, therefore, called upon to be a bulwark against corruption, injustice, misery and pain in this world. The church that only considers its own interests cannot be called a church of Christ anymore. Church councils and other governing bodies of every denomination have to keep this principle in mind whenever they take decisions and decide how to spend their funds.

Involvement in the Lives of Christians
When Cain killed his brother Abel, the Lord came to him and asked: "Where is Abel, your brother?" Cain answered, "I don`t know. Am I my brother`s keeper?" (Gen 4: 9).

The answer to Cain's question is a definite 'Yes'. We certainly are our brothers' and sisters' keepers.

It is the task of the elders and other leaders in the church to administer discipline where members act immorally or illegally. Jesus gave us clear prescriptions how people who sin deliberately are to be dealt with (Matt 18: 15–20). They are initially to be confronted during a pastoral conversation in which they must be shown in a loving manner that their behavior does not befit a child of God. If that does not help, they are to be admonished by more than one person in a leadership position. Should that not bring the desired results about that person has to be reported to the church council and fitting measures should be decided upon.

We must remember that the church is a voluntary organization and no church council has the authority to punish people by forcing them to pay a fine or obliging them to do community service or something similar. Members of the church are supposed to adhere willingly to all biblical principles and they are to be lovingly convinced of their wrong-doing, should that come to light. If that person refuses to be convinced, then he may – eventually – be disciplined by treating him as if he is "a Gentile or a tax collector". That means that such a person may be regarded as a non-believer and his membership may be declared to have ended. In other words – that person may be banned from the Christian community.

This all boils down to the fact that it is part of the management of the church that wrong-doing and sin cannot be condoned, because Christians are supposed to lead exemplary lives.

Examples of Good Managers in the Bible

There are various examples of good managers in the Bible and it will be profitable to have a look at their management styles:

- *Joseph:* This Hebrew man found favor with the king of Egypt and he rose to the position of prime minister and minister of agriculture. Egypt is dependent upon the Nile that overflowed its banks during the rainy season in parts of Africa to the south. Sometimes the rain stayed away and the Nile did not overflow – leaving the farmers along its banks without irrigation water. Joseph ordered storage depots to be constructed where the surplus of good years could be stored for meagre years. This is a good example of good management – making provision for unforeseen problems.

- *Moses:* He had to lead a bunch of former slaves through the desert and forge them into a society with laws and rules and to transform them into the people of God. He also appointed group leaders to deal with less serious issues because he was overwhelmed by taking responsibility for solving all problems. This illustrates the principle that no organization – including the church – can operate and survive without discipline and the delegation of tasks.

- *Nehemiah:* This Jew was appointed governor of Judea by the king of Persia. He found Jerusalem full of demoralized people due to the perilous state of the city walls, which invited looters and enemies to take advantage of this state of affairs. He managed to motivate the people to cooperate in rebuilding the walls. He is a good example of a manager who succeeded in motivating people to work together on an important task.

- *Jesus:* Jesus trained a dozen men from various backgrounds – fishermen, tax collectors, former terrorists and tradesmen – to become his apostles after his departure. It is clear from this example that no Christian leader can hope to achieve results without training his followers and developing their skills.

3. CHURCH LEADERSHIP ACCORDING TO THE NEW TESTAMENT

Read: Is 22: 15 –21; 1 Tim 3: 1–13; 5: 17–20.
What are the requirements for people who serve in positions of leadership or an official capacity in the church?

Read: Acts 20: 17 & 28; Phil 1: 1; Eph 4: 11; 1 Tim 3: 1–2; 3: 8; 5: 17.
What types of leaders does the church need?

Read: Acts 6: 1–6; 14: 23
How are leaders in the church to be chosen or appointed?

The Job of the Pastor/Minister/Priest
People sometimes think that a pastor/minister/priest has a very nice job. He lives in the church's house without paying rent, receives a sizable salary and only works on a Sunday. That is, however, not quite how things are in reality. The job of a pastor/minister/priest is usually very stressful, due to the following reasons:

The job of the pastor/minister/priest is –

- Impossible;
- Frustrating; but also
- The most wonderful job in the world.

The pastor has to do a delicate balancing act;
- He must keep the congregation happy; and –
- He must keep his own family happy.

Both can only be achieved through the grace of God.

Offices in the New Testament

There was no uniform system of church offices or officials at the time of the New Testament. Different groups of biblical writings knew different types of offices or officials.

The *Pauline Epistles* are the eldest part of the New Testament; they were written during the fifties and early sixties of the first century AD. Paul mentions the following services or offices:

- Servant (διακονος – *diakonos*)
- Overseer (ἔπισκοπος – *episkopos*) – supervisor or bishop
- Apostle (missionary)
- Evangelist
- Prophet
- Shepherd
- Teacher
- Deacon (διακονος – *diakonos*)

The *Pastoral Epistles* (1 and 2 Timothy and Titus) were written on behalf of the apostle Paul by an unknown secretary. The following services or offices are mentioned:

- Apostle (missionary)
- Overseer (ἔπισκοπος – *episkopo*s) – supervisor or bishop. They and the elders were actually the same office or service.
- Elder (πρεσβυτερος – *presbuteros*). The name or title of "priest" was derived from this title.
- Deacon (διακονος – *diakonos*)
- Widow (most probably a female elder or deacon)
- Servant (διακονος – *diakonos*)
- Teacher

The *Synoptic Gospels* (Mark, Matthew and Luke) and *Acts* were compiled after the fall of Jerusalem and the destruction of the temple during the Jewish War against the Romans (AD 67–70). These documents list the following officials:

- Teacher
- Prophet
- Apostle (a member of the group of 12)
- Servant (διακονος – *diakonos*)
- Elder (πρεσβυτερος – *presbuteros*)
- Shepherd

The book of *Hebrews* only mentions "leaders" (13: 7, 17 & 24).

In the *Gospel and Epistles of John* (written during the nineties of the first century AD) one finds the following names for officials:

- Prophet
- Teacher
- Shepherd
- Servant (διακονos – diakonos)

The book of *Revelation* (about AD 96) knew of the following titles for church leaders:

- Prophet
- Apostle
- Angel/messenger

What is an Office in the Church?
It is clear from the preceding that there was a wide variety of names for people who served in an official capacity in the church during

the first century AD. One can summarize the following characteristics of all these services or offices:

- Jesus Christ is the prototype of a church official in his capacity as King, Prophet and Priest.
- There were variations between the different parts of the New Testament – initially the functions and roles were rather informal, but they got more formalized as time went on.
- A church official must be somebody who is called by God or Christ to this office.
- The Holy Spirit provided the necessary spiritual gifts to people serving in the above positions.
- People who served in these positions had to lead blameless lives.
- All these functions or services functioned exclusively within the local church; even Paul, the apostle, was a teacher in the church of Antioch, which sent him out as a missionary (Acts 13: 1–3). After his travels, he reported back to the church of Antioch (Acts 14: 27).
- The New Testament is adamant that all believers are equal because they are all children of God. There are, however, leaders needed to guide the church in accordance with the teachings and principles of the Word of God.
- These officials were serving leaders, but also leading servants. The New Testament, strictly speaking, does not use the term "official" – all the "officials" were actually "servants" (διακονοι – *diakonoi*). There were no "offices" – only "services".
- These leaders or servants came together in meetings to take decisions regarding the well-being or actions of their flocks; all

members of the congregations or local churches were often allowed to participate in deliberations (Acts 15).

Servants and not Rulers

Followers of Jesus Christ who performed some or other function in the church, *served* in those positions. They served God, but also their fellow believers and their fellow human beings. An official position was, therefore, not a way to get rich or to gain a position of authority or influence over others.

It will be good to be reminded of the following words of Jesus:

> "But don`t you be called `Rabbi,` for one is your teacher, the Christ, and all of you are brothers. Call no man on the earth your father, for one is your Father, he who is in heaven. Neither be called masters, for one is your master, the Christ. But he who is greatest among you will be your servant" (Matt 8: 8–11).

We also read:

> "Then came to him the mother of the sons of Zebedee with her sons, kneeling and asking a certain thing of him. He said to her, 'What do you want?' She said to him, 'Command that these, my two sons, may sit, one on your right hand, and one on your left hand, in your kingdom.' (....) When the ten heard it, they were moved with indignation concerning the two brothers. But Jesus called them to him, and said, 'You know that the rulers of the Gentiles lord it over them, and their great ones exercise authority over them. It shall not be so among you, but whoever would become great among you will be your servant'" (Matt 20: 20–26).

Unfortunately, the history of Christianity contains numerous examples of church officials who abused their positions to amass riches or to become secular rulers. This was especially true of the Roman Catholic popes and bishops during the Middle Ages and the Renaissance. Many of them lived in luxurious palaces and also held the title of prince or something similar. For instance, the prime minister of King Louis XIV of France was Cardinal Richelieu, a senior church official; he ran the country on behalf of the king. The present pope, Francis, however, provides a wonderful example of humility and service to others.

In their capacity as servants of God and the church, all these various officials are called to provide leadership. This has, of course, to be performed in accordance with the Gospel of Jesus Christ.

4. THE TASKS AND ROLES OF MINISTERS OR PASTORS

Read: 1 Cor 12: 28–30

What types of activities were performed by leaders in the Christian community in Paul's time?

The minister, priest or pastor of a church has the task of being the spiritual leader of the congregation. This task has many facets.

The training of the spiritual leaders of the church must equip these leaders for multiple tasks and roles and it usually takes a number of years. The following tasks and roles have traditionally been associated with the position or office of the pastor or priest:

Preaching

This is the most visible aspect of the pastor, priest or minister's work. The congregation assembles on the Lord's Day specifically for the purpose of being fed spiritually from the Word of God and it is the task of the preacher to explain a certain text in Holy Scripture and apply it to current circumstances.

Paul advised his pupil Timothy with the following words:

"I charge you therefore before God and the Lord, Jesus Christ, who will judge the living and the dead at His appearing and His kingdom: preach the word; be urgent in season and out of season; reprove, rebuke, and exhort, with all patience and teaching" (2 Tim 4: 1–2).

Justin Martyr, a theologian of the second century, wrote in Ch 67 of his First Apology (ca AD 155) about the practice in early Christianity to listen to sermons on the Lord's Day:

"And on the day called Sunday, all who live in cities or in the country gather together to one place, and the memoirs of the apostles or the writings of the prophets are read, as long as time permits; then, when the reader has ceased, the president verbally instructs, and exhorts to the imitation of these good things."

This task of preaching is related to that of the prophet. It is expected of a prophet to proclaim God's will to mankind, to explain the message of the Bible and to warn people to turn to God (Rev 1: 3; Rev 13: 7; Rev 22: 7, 9–10 & 18–19). Whenever a preacher ascends a pulpit to deliver a sermon, he also acts as a prophet.

Administering the Sacraments

Whenever a pastor, priest or minister is ordained – that is, receiving the authority and competence to fulfill the tasks and duties connected to that office or service – the authority to administer the sacraments is conveyed upon that person. That means that he may baptize new members of the congregation and officiate at the Lord's Supper or Eucharist.

Jesus gave the following order to his apostles upon his ascension into heaven: "Go, and make disciples of all nations, baptizing them in the name of the Father and of the Son and of the Holy Spirit" (Matt 28: 19).

Acts 2: 46 reports that the first Christians were "breaking bread at home" – that is, celebrating the Eucharist in the homes of members of the community because there were no church buildings at that time. This happened under the supervision of the apostles.

Providing Pastoral Care

Through the ages, it was always the task of the pastor to provide comfort and support to those who were in mourning after the death of a loved one, the sick, the elderly, the destitute and the lonely. The pastor had to aid those who struggled with life problems and spiritual problems.

The word "pastor" is the Latin for "shepherd". Jesus provided the example by calling himself the "Good Shepherd" (John 10: 1-16). Paul told the elders of the church in Ephesus: "Take heed, therefore, to yourselves, and to all the flock, in which the Holy Spirit has made you overseers, to shepherd the assembly of the Lord and God which he purchased with his own blood" (Acts 20: 28).

Providing Moral Leadership

We unfortunately live in a world filled with temptations, leading to crime, injustice, marital unfaithfulness, lies, cheating and corruption. The temptation is always there for a minister, priest or pastor to become involved in questionable practices and schemes. Giving in to these temptations will inevitably lead to his downfall.

In his first letter to Timothy and his letter to Titus, the apostle Paul gave a detailed account of the moral qualities desired of church leaders. It is clear that they have to be moral examples, above reproach and shining lights in a dark world. They have the example of Jesus whose conduct was always above criticism.

This all means that spiritual leaders have the task to promote that which is good and right and to fight that which is bad and wrong. There are clear relevant guidelines in the Bible. Values such as honesty, integrity, truthfulness, transparency, reliability, compassion and empathy are to be found on more or less every page of Holy Scripture.

Teaching

Ministers or priests are often called "teachers" in the New Testament (Acts 13: 1; Rom 12: 7; 1 Cor 12: 28; Eph 4: 11).

Teaching and preaching are certainly related, but they are not quite the same activity. When the pastor teaches his flock, he is instructing them in the mysteries of the Word of God, on how to answer the arguments of those who do not believe and how to be witnesses for Jesus Christ. Teaching is especially directed towards new members of the congregation and younger persons.

Preaching is primarily an act of motivation. Teaching is an act of spreading knowledge.

Studying

Jesus called his followers "disciples". This word means "apprentice" or "pupil". He trained them by his example and by his lessons to carry on his work after his death.

Every priest, minister or pastor, needs constant training to be able to perform his tasks diligently. The congregation actually pays the spiritual leader a salary or a stipend to enable him to provide spiritual guidance to the members of the congregation. For that, the spiritual leader has to be an expert on the Bible, theological questions and matters relating to the church. That is only possible if he continues to be a disciple of Jesus by studying and broadening his knowledge. Without studying the preacher will run out of ideas to proclaim from the pulpit and perform his task as a teacher.

Personal Devotions

A task that is connected to that of studying is the task of setting time aside for personal devotions – Bible study and prayer. The pastor, minister or priest who neglects this task and doesn't grow spiritually, can't be a proper spiritual guide for his followers in the congregation.

Evangelism

The book of Acts in the New Testament contains the story of how the apostles and their helpers spread the message about Jesus Christ. It started in Jerusalem after the outpouring of the Holy Spirit (Acts 2). Those who accepted this message were baptized and organized into a community. The message was carried to neighboring towns and cities – even as far as Damascus (Acts 2: 41-47). After his conversion, the apostle Paul undertook extensive travels throughout the Greek-speaking world in Asia Minor, the islands of the Mediterranean, Greece and eventually Italy. He founded churches wherever he convinced people to embrace Jesus Christ as their Savior.

Jesus gave this last instruction to his disciples before He was taken up into heaven: "But you will receive power when the Holy Spirit has come on you. You will be witnesses to me in Jerusalem, in all Judea and Samaria, and to the uttermost parts of the earth" (Acts 1: 8).

Management, Organization and Administration

This manual deals extensively with this aspect of the task of the priest, pastor or minister.

Representing the Congregation in the Community

The pastor is usually the spokesperson for his congregation. Whenever the news media want to know about a certain event or development in a certain congregation or church, they usually contact the pastor who is supposed to know all about the event or development.

The minister, priest or pastor is in a certain sense the "face" and the "voice" of the congregation. He is the person who provides spiritual leadership by formulating the vision, mission and motto of the congregation and providing a decisive influence in the culture of the congregation. It often happens that people travel some distance away from their homes to attend a certain church because they feel at home in that church and that is mostly due to the atmosphere created by the spiritual leader of that church or congregation.

Community Service
The church is part of civil society. There are various organizations in our communities dealing with social issues, such as child abuse, animal rights, providing shelter to the homeless, counselling helpless people, rehabilitation of alcoholics and drug addicts, *etcetera*. These projects deserve the support of all well-meaning citizens, including members of the churches. Pastors, priests and ministers – who are the faces and voices of their churches – ought to show an example to their parishioners by becoming involved in these projects. Where they help to fight injustice and crime and endeavor to further that which is right and good, they are serving the interests of the Kingdom of Heaven.

5. WOMEN IN LEADERSHIP POSITIONS

Read: Gen 1: 27; Gen 2: 22-24
Are men superior beings in comparison to women?

Many churches are of the opinion that it is against the teachings of the Bible to appoint women as ministers, priests, bishops, elders or deacons. They usually base this conviction on the following arguments:

Jesus' Disciples were Men

It is true that Jesus chose twelve men to be his disciples or apostles. They were the first leaders of the Christian community in Jerusalem (Acts 2: 42). The apostles were joined by seven men who had the task of caring for Greek-speaking widows and orphans (Acts 6: 1–6).

Jesus selected exactly twelve men to be his disciples since they symbolized the twelve patriarchs and tribes of the people of Israel from the Old Testament. Jesus meant that the body of his followers would be a continuation of the people of God from the Old Testament. To his disciples He declared: "Most assuredly I tell you, that you who have followed me, in the regeneration when the Son of Man will sit on the throne of his glory, you also will sit on twelve thrones, judging the twelve tribes of Israel" (Matt 19: 28).

It would never have made sense to Jesus' contemporaries if He had appointed women to this group of twelve apostles as representatives of the ancient patriarchs and tribes of Israel.

1 Cor 14: 33–35

In this passage, it is written:

> "As in all the assemblies of the saints, let your women keep silence in the assemblies, for it is not permitted for them to speak; but let them be in subjection, as the Law also says. If they desire to learn anything, let them ask their own husbands at home, for it is shameful for a woman to chatter in the assembly."

There are clear indications that this passage was not written by Paul but added by a scribe who copied the manuscripts of the first letter to the Corinthians and who wanted to insert his ideas about the inferior status of women into the manuscript. This passage, therefore, does not belong in the Bible.

This passage is, moreover, directly contradicted by 1 Cor 11: 5–6 where Paul found it quite in order for women to pray and prophesy in the assembly, provided they were properly clothed as befitting a chaste Christian woman:

> "But every woman praying or prophesying with her head unveiled dishonors her head. For it is one and the same thing as if she were shaved. For if a woman is not covered, let her also be shorn. But if it is shameful for a woman to be shorn or shaved, let her be covered."

1 Tim 2: 11–12

This passage is also quoted by those who are against the ordination of women:

> "Let a woman learn in quietness with all subjection. But I don't permit a woman to teach, nor to exercise authority over a man, but to be in quietness."

This passage is usually translated incorrectly. It does not mean that all women are subjected to all men. Where Paul wrote that a woman ought not to exercise "authority over a man" it should actually be translated that no woman should exercise authority over her *own* husband – not men in general.

In Eph 5: 21 Paul clearly advised a married couple that they ought to have the attitude of "subjecting yourselves one to another in the fear of Christ." He also taught in Gal 3: 28 that social distinctions did not apply in the Christian assembly: "There is neither Jew nor Greek, there is neither slave nor free man, there is neither male nor female; for you are all one in Christ Jesus."

In other words: although women were expected to respect their husbands, that injunction applied equally to the attitude of husbands towards their wives. They are equals.

Examples of Women in Positions of Leadership

There are various examples of women who held positions of leadership in the early church and it is nowhere stated that this was an undesirable state of affairs. The best-known missionary couple in the New Testament was undoubtedly Priscilla and Aquila. Their names occur six times in Acts and the letters of Paul. It is remarkable that the name of Priscilla is mentioned in three cases before that of her husband – which is an indication that she was actually the leading figure in the couple (Acts 18: 2, 18 & 26; Rom 16: 3; 1 Cor 16:19; 2 Tim 4:19).

In Rom 16: 1-2 Paul recommends Phoebe, "who is a servant of the assembly that is at Cenchreae," to the recipients of his letter in Rome. The word" servant" is a mistranslation. This woman was actually a deacon and she was in charge of those who provided lodgings to visiting Christians.

Paul greets "Andronicus and Junias, my relatives and my fellow prisoners, who are notable among the apostles" in Rom 16: 7. This is another mistranslation. No male from antiquity ever carried the name of Junias. The correct translation of this name is "Junia" – clearly a woman's name. According to Paul, she and her companion Andronicus were notable apostles.

Paul mentions in Rom 16 four other women who were his co-missionaries: Mary. Tryphaena, Tryphosa and Persis (Rom 16: 6 & 12).

Two women, Euodia and Syntiche, are mentioned in Phil 4: 2–3 as colleagues of Paul as missionaries.

In 1 Tim 3: 11 Paul names the qualities required of female deacons. Most translations make of these women the wives of deacons, but that is not what the text in Greek says. It is quite clear that female deacons are being meant.

Paul describes in 1 Tim 5: 9–19 the office of a widow – the female counterpart of the office of elder:

> "Let none be enrolled as a widow under sixty years old, having been the wife of one man, well reported of for good works; if she has brought up children, if she has used hospitality to strangers, if she has washed the saints` feet, if she has relieved the afflicted, if she has diligently followed every good work."

All these quotations from the New Testament clearly show that there were women who held positions of leadership in the church as apostles, missionaries, female elders and female deacons. Paul held them in high regard and he never gave an indication that it was wrong that they performed these functions in the church. If it was a mistake, he would never have described the desired qualities of female elders and female deacons.

6. QUALITIES OF GOOD SPIRITUAL LEADERS

Read: 1 Tim 3

What are the requirements for people in leadership positions in the church?

What is expected from a good pastor, minister or priest (and elder or deacon)? Research has highlighted the following qualities:

Personality Traits

Pastors should have the following personality traits:

- *Firmness of principle*: It is expected that the pastor should be a shining example of ethical and moral behavior. He should have a fixed set of moral principles to which he adheres. These principles should include the principle that the help-seeker's well-being must be promoted, that no illegal activities should be undertaken and that the interests and rights of all people should be protected (1 Tim 3).
- *Honesty and credibility*: The pastor must be himself. It doesn't work to try to be someone he cannot be since that is not sincere. Everything the pastor says must be true and credible.
- *Good social adjustment*: It goes without saying that a pastor must be a mature, well-balanced person without any serious personality flaws. A person with a personality disorder, a mood disorder or an addiction simply isn't suited to be a pastor (Matt 24: 45 – 53).

- *Devotion to duty*: A lazy and careless person won't be able to look after the interests of others or the flock of the Lord (Matt 24: 45 – 53).
- *Friendliness and approachability*: A sour, unapproachable and unfriendly person will repel members of the congregation and potential help-seekers.
- *Courtesy*: Good manners always make a good impression. Nobody trusts a loud–mouthed, rude and bossy person, although such a person may sometimes be popular within certain circles.
- *Marital faithfulness*: The care–giving situation creates intimacy between pastor and help–seeker. Personal information is often discussed. There is always the danger of sexual attraction developing between people of opposite sexes in such a situation. The pastor should never give in to these temptations and stay faithful to his spouse.

These personality traits can be nursed and developed; they are not necessarily fixed for time and eternity.

Motivation

If a person has no desire to be a pastor or pastoral care-giver then help-seekers will sooner or later find this out and go out of that person's way. How must the motivation of a pastor be?

- *Self-motivation*: The pastor should be a self-motivated person who doesn't need to be ordered or forced to do something. He must be able to take the initiative, especially in crisis situations.
- *A strong commitment to the interests of God's Kingdom*: The pastor should see himself primarily as a servant of God. That means that the interests of the Kingdom of God should be promoted, also when dealing with help-seekers (Rom 1: 1).

- *Obedience to the prescriptions of the Bible*: The pastor is a servant of God. That means that the servant should be obedient to the teachings of Jesus and the apostles.

Abilities and Skills:

Pastors should have certain abilities and skills which can be taught:

- *Self–confidence when dealing with others*: The pastor must be able to speak without fear for ridicule and with conviction.
- *Knowledge of the Bible*: Many help–seekers need information about God, Jesus Christ or the Christian way of life. The pastor should know his Bible well enough to provide answers.
- *Good social skills*: The pastor should know how to deal with people in different situations – especially people who experience problems of a spiritual or psychological nature.
- *Job satisfaction*: The role of minister, priest or pastor is not a "job" in the ordinary sense of the word, it is rather a calling or a vocation. To fulfill this role effectively and efficiently the pastor should enjoy doing this "work" and deriving pleasure from it. It always gives humble satisfaction when a person who lives under a cloud starts to smile and experiences hope when aided by the pastor. We may be sure that Jesus felt this satisfaction many times in his dealings with sinners.

7. THE STRUCTURE OF THE CHURCH

Read: Acts 20: 17 & 28–30; Phil 1: 1–2
By whom is the management and administration of a local church to be performed?

Read: Acts 13: 1–3; 14: 27; 15: 2 & 30
Is there a place for official meetings of the whole congregation? Is this necessary?

Read: Acts 15: 2 & 23–29; 2 Cor 8: 1–5; 8: 18–19 & 23
Is it necessary for churches to cooperate with each other? How do they do that?

When the word "church" (Greek: ʼεκκλήσια – *ekklesia*) is encountered in the New Testament, it may mean one of two things:

- The local church; in other words, the congregation or parish; or
- The universal Church, the church in its totality, consisting of all believers on earth, past and present

Church Councils

During his missionary travels, the apostle Paul established churches in various cities in the Greek world: Corinth, Ephesus, Philippi, Thessalonica and elsewhere. He afterwards wrote letters to some of those churches. He also wrote a letter to the Christians in Rome, the capital of the Roman Empire. We don't know who established that church, but by the time Paul wrote his letter, he knew of quite a number of Christians there to whom he sent greetings (Rom 16: 1–16).

Paul's colleague, Titus, founded churches on the island of Crete where he had to appoint elders in the various towns (Tit 1: 5–9).

All churches in the time of the apostles were managed and administered by a church council, consisting of a number of elders and deacons who were appointed by the congregations (Acts 14: 23; Phil 1: 1–2). The first congregation in Jerusalem was initially administered by the group of twelve apostles (Acts 2: 43–47). When the numbers of believers grew a group of seven men were chosen to run affairs (Acts 6: 1–7). It is often asserted that these men were deacons, although that title is not used to describe them in Acts 6. In Acts 11: 28 and 15: 2, 13 & 22 one suddenly finds a council of elders of which James, the brother of Jesus, was chairman; they managed affairs in the congregation in conjunction with the apostles who acted as preachers. We don't read in Acts when exactly these elders were chosen. It is reasonable to suppose that the seven men chosen in Acts 6 were actually these elders. After all, the Jewish synagogues in those days were also managed by a council of seven elders and it is safe to accept that the first Christian congregation followed this example.

The requirements for elders and deacons are given in 1 Tim 3: 1–13 and Tit 1: 6–9. They were required to be people with unblemished records, exemplary behavior and a sound faith. The seven men chosen according to Acts 6 had to be filled with the Spirit and possess wisdom.

Superior Meetings

The various churches through the Mediterranean region that were established through the missionary work of the apostles and other missionaries were bound together by their common faith in Jesus Christ. They also kept contact with each other. In his first letter to the church in Corinth, Paul sent greetings to the Christians in this city on behalf of "the churches in the province of Asia" (1 Cor 16: 19). When Paul was in Corinth and he wrote his letter to the Christians in Rome, he greeted a number of friends and acquaintances by name and he also sent greetings on behalf of "all the churches of Christ" (Acts 16: 1–16). He must have had a mandate from these churches to do so. Paul organized a charity drive for the impoverished Christians in Jerusalem and got the cooperation of various other churches for this project (2 Cor 8: 16–23).

When the Christians in Antioch became confused regarding the requirement propagated by certain Jewish Christians that all believers had to be circumcised, it was decided to send a delegation to Jerusalem to consult with the apostles and elders there on this matter (Acts 15: 1–2). This is the first known case where delegates from more than one church came together to discuss spiritual and doctrinal issues. This set the example through the ages for councils, synods, conferences and other gatherings where deputies of various churches met to deliberate on various matters regarding the management and administration of the churches that participated.

Every congregation or local church is a complete church and should not be seen as a "branch" of the larger denomination. The reason for this is that the individual churches founded during the time of the apostles were initially separate and independent entities. They only formed associations with each other as time went on.

A denomination consists of a number of congregations or churches that are bound together by a common faith or doctrine and system of church governance. All participating churches have the capacity to manage their own affairs and make decisions regarding all issues that affect them. When a number of churches of the same denomination get together in a classis, circuit, conference, general meeting, council or synod when their delegates constitute a meeting, these gatherings may only discuss general issues that affect all the participating churches. These gatherings may only interfere in the internal workings of individual churches when it becomes clear that malpractices and maladministration occur or that another state of emergency arose.

Although many denominations regard these gatherings of delegates as standing or permanent bodies, it must be stated that such meetings actually ought to disband when their work is done. That is what happened in the case of the meeting described in Acts 15. The denomination as a collection or grouping of local churches, of course, stays in existence. Its governing body, the classis, circuit, conference, synod, council or whatever it is called, has to be constituted anew every time a new meeting is called. The only permanent bodies are the church councils of the various congregations.

A superior meeting, be it a council, synod or conference, is not more important than a church council. Church councils may deliberate on anything pertaining to the church, whereas superior meetings may only discuss issues that affect all the participating churches collectively. Church councils are permanent bodies, while superior meetings disband after having concluded their business. The chairperson of a superior meeting also does not hold a permanent position; that position has to be filled anew at the start of every new meeting. It is, therefore, wrong to speak of "the moderator of the church" or a similar position. That person was merely the chairperson of the previous meeting of the synod or whatever superior meeting. It is also wrong to think that a circuit meeting, synod or council goes into "recess" after having concluded its business, as if it were a permanent body, such as a parliament or a board of directors of a company.

Some denominations have the habit of appointing their pastor or minister as a permanent chairperson of the church council. If there is more than one pastor or minister in that church, they have to rotate that position. Other denominations choose a new chairperson of the church council every year from the ministers and elders.

8.   THE CHURCH AS AN ORGANIZATION

Read: 1 Cor 1: 10–17; 1 Cor 12: 12–13 & 27–30; Col 1: 18
What does the apostle Paul expect from the church and its members?

There can be no doubt that the local church or a congregation is an organization. To understand the church, it is necessary to investigate what the Bible tells us in this regard since Christians insist that the church ought to be structured according to biblical principles. It is also necessary to have a look at the church from the perspective of organizational theory in order to make out which role the church plays as a social organization in the lives of people and to identify mistakes that have to be avoided.

The congregation as a system/organization
What is an organization? Schein has this definition:

> "An organization is the planned co-ordination of the activities of a number of people for the achievement of some common, explicit purpose or goal, through division of labour and function, and through a hierarchy of authority and responsibility." [1]

Tosi *et al.* give the following definition:

> "An organization is a group of people working toward objectives that develops and maintains stable and predictable behavior patterns."[2]

---

[1] Schein\, *Organizational Psychology*, 15.

[2] Tosi *et al.*, *Managing Organizational Behavior,* 39.

These definitions are also applicable to churches/congregations.
Organizations exhibit certain characteristics:

- An organization is an open system, which interacts with its environment.
- An organization can have more than one function or goal.
- An organization is constituted by a number of subsystems; these subsystems exist in dynamic interaction with each other. An organization is not a collection of individual people but a collection of subsystems: coalitions, groups, teams and roles.
- Subsystems are mutually dependent; changes in one influence the behaviour of the others.
- The environment of an organization is constituted by other systems that pose demands on it or create limitations on it.
- Because of the dynamic interaction between an organization and its environment the border between the two is very often vague, changing or fuzzy.
- The processes going on inside an organization – input, processing and output – tell us more about the type of organization we deal with than its size, form or design.[3]

Everything that has been said about organizations in general is also applicable to a church/congregation (Schein, 1988: 12, 13). A local church or congregation/parish is a dynamic system of which the different subsystems have to co-operate smoothly. Conflict is always bad. There has to be a clear division of roles and the members have to support each other.

There are different types of organizations. According to Schein there are four types:

---

[3] Schein, *Organizational Psychology*, 228–29.

- Businesses – their goal is to produce profits and to benefit the management and owners/shareholders (example: all the organizations that are trying to make a profit);
- Service organizations – their goal is to provide services to their clients (example: welfare societies);
- Utility organizations – their goal is to benefit the public at large (example: public authorities);
- Organizations for mutual benefit – their goal is to provide benefit to their members.[4]

The church is an example of the last two types of organizations. It can only stay afloat if it provides in the needs of its members and promotes their interests[5], as well as performing a useful function in society.

Churches can also be seen as *voluntary organizations*. This type of organization endeavours to provide in some or other public need and is constituted of people who join voluntarily. It is not possible to enforce discipline by means of force or the withholding of benefits; the organization has to rely on the members' loyalty and value systems for their co-operation.[6]

Organizational structures

Every organization – the church included – has some or other structure. The structure determines the relationships between the members and the tasks they perform; these relationships regulate matters such as job/task differentiation, policies, authority, roles, control and co-ordination[7]. The organization exists independently of

---

[4] Schein, *Organizational Psychology*, 33.

[5] Schein, *Organizational Psychology*, 33

[6] Pattison, *Pastor and Parish,* 8–10).

[7] Tosi *et al.*, *Managing Organizational Behavior,* 39.

its members. The people come and go but the organization retains its identity. The organization will only change if the relationships between the activities and roles within change[8]

Organizations are usually comprised of the following components: goals, structures, people, information, communication channels, awards, tasks/roles and an environment.[9] This is also true of a church. As a social system the church has the following subsystems: the pastor(s), the church council, the members who may or may not join certain groups (examples: Bible study groups, the church choir etc) and the environment. Usually, the church also has a constitution, which regulates its activities and structure. Churches also have creeds – documents in which their faith is systematically formulated and it is expected of all officials and members to adhere to it. The church is a dynamic system, which is greater than the sum total of its constituent parts.[10]

Brekke *et al.* wrote:

"The whole ministry of the church is a process of interaction between pastor and people, between individual members and all the people whose lives they touch, between pastors, between church members..."[11]

The environment of a church comprises the community or society in which it is situated, other churches of the same denomination, other denominations and government structures with their laws, regulations and rules. There has to be a clear demarcation between any church and its environment but, on the other hand, it is necessary

---

[8] Schein, *Organizational Psychology*, 16.

[9] Hall, "The Effect of the Individual: 15.

[10] Martens, *Die Rol van die Predikant* 29, 33).

[11] Brekke *et al. Ten Faces of Ministry,* 20.

that the church fits in well within its environment, without acting against its own principles.

Clashes of interest between churches and their environments are sometimes inevitable, but when that leads to hostility it may be detrimental for the church. Fortunately, most countries subscribe to the principles of freedom of religion, opinion and conscience, together with freedom of association, which means that authorities will not unnecessarily get involved in the inner workings of churches – unless these churches act unlawfully.

The Functions of an Organization

In order to continue its existence an organization must have some or other helpful or beneficial function. The church can be classified as an organization for mutual benefit. That means that it has the function to exist for the benefit of its members and to serve the interests of its members – as seen from the perspective organizational theory.[12] From a biblical point of view, the function of the church is, of course, to serve as the body of Christ on earth and to promote the interests of God's Kingdom.

The effectiveness of an organization is dependent on the following factors:

- *Productivity* – every member must render a constructive contribution;
- *The satisfaction of the members* – their needs must be met [inter alia, their need for identity, stimulation, security, freedom and responsibility, and meaning – more about this later when motivation is discussed];
- *Attendance* – members must be willing and prepared to be present;

---

[12] Schein, *Organizational Psychology*, 33.

- *Retention* – members must be retained and there must be a low turnover;
- *Adaptation* – members must be willing to learn new ideas, attitudes and behaviour to adapt to new conditions;
- *Physical and psychological welfare* – membership of the group must serve the benefit of the members and further their interests.[13]

The health and effectiveness of an organization – the church included – can be measured against the following criteria:

- *Adaptability* – there must the ability to address problems and to react effectively to the claims and challenges of the environment;
- *A sense of identity* – the members must agree about the goals, values, culture and task of the organization;
- *Ability to test reality* – the environment must be perceived and interpreted accurately in order to identify the demands from the environment;
- *Integration* – the subsystems in the organization must co-operate as a unity.[14] These criteria also apply to a congregation. If there is a lack of unity, co-operation, mutual goals and values the congregation will function badly.[15]

There is a so-called *psychological contract* between any organization and its members. The organization, as well as its members, must benefit from their relationship. Both may have certain expectations of the other. The members, on the one hand, are

---

[13] Tosi *et al.*, *Managing Organizational Behavior,* 5–6, 377–78.

[14] Schein, *Organizational Psychology,* 232.

[15] Martens, *Die Rol van die Predikant,* 31–35.

interested in the satisfaction of their needs and respect for their rights and privileges as members.

The organization, on the other hand, is interested in the service the members can render, their loyalty, motivation and the furtherance of the interests of the organization. The organization may expect that the members work hard and be productive, that they don't waste time and utilise resources optimally.[16]

All these principles also apply to the church. A congregation can only flourish if it has a useful function, if it fulfils certain criteria and has a satisfactory psychological contract with its members. The pastor is a key figure in all these matters. It is largely dependent upon his endeavours if the needs of the members are being identified, if the congregation's members co-operate as a unity and whether the demands of the environment are being met.[17]

---

[16] Schein, *Organizational Psychology*, 22–23; Tosi *et al.*, *Managing Organizational Behavior*, 744; Hilliard, *Performance Improvement*, 46.

[17] Brekke *et al.*, *Ten Faces of Ministry*, 193.

9.   THE LEGAL STATUS OF THE CHURCH

Read: 1 Cor 4: 9–13; 1 Pet 4: 12–16; Rev 6:9.
Did the Christians in the apostolic age enjoy freedom of religion? How were they treated?

Freedom of Religion

The Universal Declaration of Human Rights, adopted in 1948 by the United Nations, stipulates the following:

> *Article 18*
> Everyone has the right to freedom of thought, conscience and religion; this right includes freedom to change his religion or belief, and freedom, either alone or in community with others and in public or private, to manifest his religion or belief in teaching, practice, worship and observance.

All these provisions mean that every person ought to have the freedom and the right to choose he own religious beliefs and affiliation.

This all means that the state must allow churches and other religious organizations to conduct their own internal affairs as they see fit – as long as they do not break the laws of the country or infringe upon the rights of others.

It may happen, though, that some or other aggrieved official or member of a church takes the church to court due to some or other injustice suffered. In those cases, the courts will determine whether any of the country's laws were broken in the process. The court will, however, also determine whether the particular church acted in contravention of its own constitution, rules and regulations.

After all, the constitution, rules and regulations of any voluntary organization, such as a church, amounts to a binding agreement between the organization and its members. The organization and all its members have an explicit or tacit agreement that they will all act according to those rules and every member has the right to expect that the church will also respect its own rules. If a member of the organization can prove that the church acted contrary to its own constitution, rules and regulations, then the court will most likely order the church to rectify the wrong committed and redress the injustice.

Juristic Persons

The law of most countries recognizes two types of persons:

- Natural persons; and
- Juristic persons.

Natural persons are people of flesh and blood – males and females. Juristic persons are bodies or groups comprised of a number of people, such as business entities, sports clubs, welfare organizations, state departments and voluntary organizations, such as churches. The members of a juristic person vary as time goes on, but the juristic person retains its identity.

Churches are, therefore, juristic persons and they may take part in the life of the country where they are situated. They may –

- Own property;
- Employ people;
- Open bank accounts;
- Sue natural and other juristic persons;

- Be sued by aggrieved members or others; and
- May commit themselves to contracts and agreements.

There seems to be some confusion regarding exactly who in the church may do all these things. Is the congregation or the church council the juristic person? The correct legal position is that the congregation as a whole is the juristic person and that the church council is its organ or managing board, which has the mandate to take decisions on behalf of the juristic person, the body of members.

There also seems to be confusion regarding the juristic status of denominations. Is the denomination as a whole or its governing body – the synod, council, presbytery, circuit or conference – the juristic person? The correct legal position is that these governing bodies, that are supposed to be reconstituted anew every time they hold a meeting, cannot be the juristic persons. These meetings are only the organs of the grouping of churches in a denomination and they are empowered to make decisions on behalf of the participating local churches or congregations. The denomination or grouping of local churches as such is the juristic person, which may own property, take part in the economic and legal life of the country and do everything that a juristic person is entitled to do.

It is a legal requirement that every juristic person should have a constitution. Churches generally have constitutions in the form of a book of church order, a book of church law or something similar.

It has happened that some churches registered themselves as welfare organizations or organizations without profit-seeking. In those cases, the church remains a juristic person.

There are cases known where a church building and a bank account were registered in the name of the pastor, bishop or priest. This may create problems. What happens when the pastor, bishop or priest retires or dies? Who inherits the property? Who may lay claim to the funds deposited in the church leader's name? This type of arrangement should be discouraged because it may lead to all sorts of problems and unpleasantness.

Secession from a Denomination

It has happened more than once that a certain congregation tried to secede from the denomination and keep possession of all the assets. That has led to court cases in which the courts held that those members who did not join the secessionists are to be seen as a continuation of the original congregation and that all the assets still belong to them as a congregation, however few they may be in number.

Those members who have left the denomination can, therefore, lay no claim on the assets of their previous congregation or church, although they contributed financially to the accrual of those assets.

10. CONTRACTS AND AGREEMENTS

Read: Ex 19: 3–8; Ex 20: 1–3
What can we learn from the relationship between God and his people?

Read: Matt 5: 37; James 5: 12
What is expected from Christians in these verses?

It has been shown in the previous chapter that churches can be regarded as juristic persons. They can, therefore, partake in the legal, economic and business life of the country of which they are part. They may also commit themselves to contracts and agreements.

For instance, when a certain congregation decides to build a new church building, acquire a dwelling for its pastor/priest/minister or open a bank account, then agreements or contracts with a building contractor, an estate agent or a commercial bank have to be concluded. Usually, the church council or governing body empowers one or more persons to sign these agreements on behalf of the church after having accepted the conditions in the contract. It goes without saying that these conditions may not be to the disadvantage of the congregation. After all, the church council may be spending money, money that has been entrusted to their care by the parishioners and for which they have to take responsibility.

Churches are bound to agreements and contracts, just as any other natural or juristic person. One of the axioms of jurisprudence is the Latin maxim: *pacta servanda sunt.* This means: agreements (or contracts) must be honored.

That is exactly what the Bible teaches us. God promised to be the God of Israel and He expected of his people to keep their promises towards Him as well. In the Ten Commandments (Ex 20: 1–17), He gave his people the terms of the agreement between them. But Christians are also expected to be reliable and faithful in their dealings with others and keep their promises – and through that, demonstrate that they are God's children (Luke 16: 10–12).

11. THE CONSTITUTIONS OF CHURCHES

Read: 1 Cor 14: 40
Why does a church need a constitution?

Some people have argued that it is not necessary for a church to have a constitution, a book of rules, a book of canon law or a book of church order. We have, after all – according to these people – the Bible in which we find all the principles according to which the church has to be organized and managed. A book of rules supposedly restricts the freedom of God's children.

That is not what God expects from his church. To his people of the Old Testament, the Israelites, he gave many laws, which are to be found in the first five books of the Bible. These laws prescribed, amongst others, how the religious life of Israel had to be managed. Of course, Christians cannot earn eternal life by keeping these Old Testament laws scrupulously – we can only gain heaven through the grace of God and through faith in Jesus Christ (Gal 2: 15 – 4: 7).

But Christians are also required to live exemplary lives because they love God and are thankful for his saving grace. Jesus gave us a good explanation of some of the Ten Commandments in the Sermon on the Mount (Matt 5-7) and he expected his followers to adhere to these rules. In other parts of the Gospels, we also find numerous injunctions of Jesus. The same happened in the letters of the apostle Paul. In Romans 12, for instance, he gave a number of rules for the lives of Christians and churches.

In other words: it is a good thing if a church has a constitution or church order in which a set of rules are given how the church is to be governed, administered and managed. If one should rely solely on the Bible for guidance regarding the governance of the church it might lead to misunderstandings and even quarrels. After all, people do not always interpret the Bible in the same way. It is, therefore, better to have a written document, a constitution.

This constitution constitutes an agreement between the church or denomination and its office bearers and members. It sets out what each may expect from the other and it is usually expected of office bearers and members to solemnly declare that they will obey the rules of the church. It may, likewise, be expected of the church or denomination as a whole also to adhere to these rules.

The following topics are usually covered in such a document:

- A statement that the church in question accepts the Bible as the Word of God;
- Which creeds or statements of faith the church regards as a faithful rendering of the message of the Bible;
- Requirements for membership of the church;
- The duties connected to the offices or services in the church;
- The training and admission of ministers/priests/pastors;
- The organization, powers and duties of congregational councils;
- The organization, powers and duties of the organs of the denomination – synods, councils, classes, conferences, presbyteries, circuits *etcetera*;
- Rules and guidelines for Sunday services and the administering of the sacraments;
- Discipline in the church;
- Rules for the conduct of meetings;

- The legal status of congregations and the church in a wider context as juristic persons; and
- Rules and guidelines to regulate the work of the church regarding education, missions, charity, finances and witnessing.

12.   LABOR RELATIONS IN THE CHURCH

Read: Matt 10:10; Gal 6: 6; Phil 4: 15; 2 Thess 3: 9.
What is the responsibility of the congregation towards its pastor(s)/priest(s)/ minister(s)?

Read: Eph 4: 11–13
What are the tasks of pastors/priests/ministers?

As a juristic person, the church is entitled to take people into employment: pastors/ministers/ priests, administrative staff, sextons, gardening and maintenance staff and musicians to play the church organ, *etcetera.*

Smaller congregations will not always have full-time staff to fill all these positions and the tasks connected to these positions may be performed by part-time employees or volunteers.

Should a church have paid employees it is necessary that a proper contract of employment be concluded with them. The following items are usually included in such a contract:

- The full name and address of the employer;
- The name and occupation of the employee, or a brief description of the work for which the employee is employed;
- The place of work, and, where the employee is required or permitted to work at various places, an indication of this;
- The date on which the employment began;
- The employee's ordinary hours of work and days of work;
- The employee's wage or the rate and method of calculating wages;

- The rate of pay for overtime work;
- Any other cash payments that the employee is entitled to;
- Any payment in kind that the employee is entitled to and the value of the payment in kind;
- How frequently remuneration will be paid;
- Any deductions to be made from the employee's remuneration;
- The leave to which the employee is entitled;
- The period of notice required to terminate employment, or if employment is for a specified period, the date when employment is to terminate;
- Any period of employment with a previous employer that counts towards the employee's period of employment;
- A list of any other documents that form part of the contract of employment, indicating a place that is reasonably accessible to the employee where a copy of each may be obtained.

The church council, as organ of the juristic person, the church or congregation, must also adhere to all other labor legislation. These laws are, for the most part, an embodiment of the principle of fairness, which is a definitive biblical principle as formulated in the so-called golden rule of Jesus (Matt 7: 12 & Luke 6: 31).

Labor legislation of most countries is nowadays usually available on the internet.

13. A VISION, MISSION AND SLOGAN FOR THE CHURCH

Read: Rev 3: 17

Do you think that this is a fitting slogan for a church? Give your reasons.

Read: Phil 1: 3–6

Do you think that Paul's vision regarding the church in Philippi is still useful for today?

Every church should have clarity about the reason for its existence, the tasks that await it and the policies to be followed. That means that every church ought to have a vision statement, a mission statement and a slogan.

A vision statement is a formulation of why the church exists and what it sees as its role in future – the dream it pursues. This vision is mostly the brain child of the pastor who is the spiritual leader of the congregation. People buy into a vision if they buy into the leader. If they trust the leader, they will also automatically trust his vision.

We may say in general that every church is supposed to serve the interests of the Kingdom of God and to continue with the work that Jesus started during his ministry on earth. The circumstances and challenges of no two churches are identical and, therefore, it is necessary to formulate a vision statement for each individual church.

An example of a vision statement may, perhaps, read as follows: "We, the Children of God in XXX (name of church), believe that the interests of God's Kingdom have to be served in our community and that we strive to be shining lights in a dark world."

The mission statement of a church gives a short explanation of what the task of that church is. Why has God called the members of this church and sent them out in the world? An example might be the following: "XXX (name of church) sees it as its mission to serve God and humanity by proclaiming the Gospel, by reaching out to those who are in need of assistance and to be a witness against injustice in this world."

Many churches also have their own slogans. Very often, it is a verse from the Bible or a summary of an important biblical principle that guides the activities of that church. An example might be: "XXX (name of the church) proclaims Christ as Savior."

All these documents will give outsiders and new members an idea of the culture and the character of that particular church.

14. LEADERSHIP STYLES

Read: Exodus 18: 11–26
Which important principles regarding leadership are to be found in this passage?

Read: Judges 7: 1–8
Why was Gideon a good leader? Give your reasons.

Managers and Leaders

Any organization – including the church – has to be managed. There must be people who provide guidance and leadership and who must be able to make decisions on a wide variety of issues. These issues will include financial expenditure, priorities in time allocation, policies to be followed, which tasks are to be performed by whom and how the organization has to be structured.

The best example of a good leader was, surely, Jesus of Nazareth. He led a group of disciples, whom he taught how to go about with their ministry. He called himself "the Good Shepherd" (John 10: 11). The name often used for a religious minister, "pastor", is the Latin word for "shepherd" and that implies that pastors, ministers and priests are supposed to follow the example of the Good Shepherd.

There is a clear relationship between the quality of leadership a pastor provides his congregation and the quality of his pastoral care. If it is apparent that he provides strong leadership on spiritual and moral issues, people will also have confidence in his ability to provide pastoral care. It is, therefore, necessary to turn our attention to the question of pastoral and moral leadership in the church.

Not every manager is necessarily a good leader, although it is possible to be both. Good managers have good control over their budgets, plan effectively, have defined goals and know how to attain those goals. They usually drive or force their subordinates to realize those goals. But that does not necessarily mean that they are also good leaders. Being a good leader entails motivating people to follow *willingly* and *voluntarily*.

Leadership may be described as follows:

"Leadership is the interpersonal influence by which one person succeeds in moving others to co-operate willingly to reach certain goals."

The Functions of Leaders

A leader must be able to perform a number of functions. He must –

- be able to provide guidance and direction;
- be able to mobilize, motivate and empower people;
- be able to help people to share in his vision for the future and to tackle the challenges connected to that; and
- help people to survive and be victorious in times of difficulty and despair.

Democratic Management Style

The current trend in the business world is to move away from management and to replace it with leadership. This also applies to the church. Members of organizations – the church included – are more sophisticated than in the past and they are more aware of their human rights. Most open and democratic societies are based on the values of human dignity, equality and freedom. The authoritarian and militaristic culture of the past is no longer acceptable and therefore the traditional style of management is increasingly being replaced by a more democratic style and structure. Members of organizations insist on being informed about the way the organization is run, and they demand greater transparency.

It is remarkable that more and more women are being appointed to management posts and senior positions. Women are less inclined than men to become aggressive and bossy and they are generally more people-orientated than men. They can thus provide the sort of leadership the world needs today.

The days of rigid organizational structures are also something of the past. It ought to be the policy of any organization to be as flexible and adaptable as possible. Organizations of the 21st century function better where responsibility and decision-making ability are spread as widely as possible – even down to the lowest levels. It should be policy to get the input of as many people as possible – recommendations, criticism and comments regarding the management of the organization. It ought to be policy to encourage all members to experiment, to innovate and to develop new systems and procedures.

It is not enough to inform members about the decisions of management or the church council; they ought to be involved in the decision-making process. Members ought to have the power to make their own decisions within the parameters of official policy. This makes a complicated system of supervision and control redundant, since members become their own supervisors and managers when they are treated as mature and responsible people.

When a church puts these principles into practice it cannot but flourish.

Inspiring Leadership

People will follow a leader if that leader has legitimacy in their eyes. This legitimacy relies on a number of factors:

- The leader must be able to exert authority by means of his personality, knowledge, skills, responsibility and integrity;
- He must be aware of his subordinates' problems and needs;
- His example must be above reproach; and
- He must have the ability to motivate and inspire others.

It goes without saying that a pastor also needs this legitimacy in order to provide good leadership.

A distinction is sometimes made between task-oriented leaders and people-oriented leaders – although a person can be both at the same time. Both styles have their place and the one does not necessarily exclude the other.

A leader with low task-orientation and low people-orientation is an ineffective and confused leader. The leader with low task-orientation and high people-orientation is a social worker rather than a leader. The leader with high task-orientation and low people-orientation is usually a weak leader and may be regarded as a mini-dictator.

Under certain circumstances, such as an emergency, it is necessary to be task-orientated. There is no time to take people's feelings into consideration or to listen to everybody's concerns and worries, as certain tasks have to be performed as quickly as possible – only the outcome counts.

Under normal circumstances, when everything is running more or less smoothly, a good leader has to be task-orientated and people-orientated at the same time. The good leader should know how people feel, think and act and he must be able to anticipate their worries and needs. In other words, the good leader knows how to motivate people by providing for their physical, psychological and spiritual needs. The good leader also knows, however, that certain tasks have to be performed and that certain goals have to be reached, which means that order and discipline have to be maintained.

Because a good leader has to be both task-orientated and people-orientated, he has to promote the welfare of his people while also seeing to it that the work is being done and that order and discipline is being preserved. It has been found that productivity is at its highest level in instances where leaders follow this double approach. If the leader is not too concerned with the interests of his people, job satisfaction will inevitably plummet and the turnover of personnel or members will be higher.

It is necessary to avoid extremes. If a supervisor scores very high on task-orientation and very low on people-orientation, productivity will fall and more complaints can be expected regarding that supervisor's dictatorial style.

To truly motivate people, as is expected of a good leader, it is necessary that people be *inspired.* A pastor is in a good position to do exactly that, since he occupies a visible leadership position and his sermons ought to motivate and inspire. If people are really inspired, then they feel enthusiastic about the attainment of a given goal and they will work diligently to reach it.

An inspiring leader needs to have integrity and to set a good example. A leader who expects others to be hard-working, honest, friendly and reliable yet does not maintain these standards himself cannot expect any results. People will rather tend to follow his bad example than to execute his orders. The result, inevitably, is low productivity.

In other words, a manager, pastor or member of the church council who acts dishonestly, untruthfully and fraudulently and who disregards his country's legislation and his church's rules will never be able to motivate others to act honestly, truthfully and reliably or to respect their country's laws and the rules of their church.

In order to be inspiring, the leader himself must be inspired and motivated. If he has a clear vision of what needs to be achieved, if he is enthusiastic about his work, if he has a passion to perform his tasks as well as possible and if he conveys the message that he is only satisfied with the highest standards, then he will be able to motive others to follow him and co-operate. This inspiration and enthusiasm cannot be anything but contagious. Such a leader will have followers rather than subordinates.

The opposite is also true. If a leader is unmotivated, lazy and slow, this example will also be contagious.

This principle can also be regarded from another angle.

There are basically three ways to control the actions of others: by using might, authority and influence.

- A leader utilizes *might* if he is in a position to reward or punish people, to impart pain or pleasure. A good example of this type of leader is the commander of a military unit.

- A leader uses *authority* if he relies on his position or rank to force people to perform certain tasks. During the industrial revolution of the nineteenth century, and also during the best part of the twentieth century, managers relied mostly on might and authority to practice control.

- Nowadays the idea has taken root that people will only be moved to do their best if leaders rely on their *influence,* derived from their personal qualities, competence and skills. If a leader is able to exert a personal and moral influence on his followers, they will follow him willingly and execute his wishes.

Good leaders also realize that the motivation of their followers is an ongoing and continuous process. People who are motivated today will not necessarily feel the same tomorrow. Any program to improve motivation must, therefore, be an ongoing process that is continuously updated and adapted. The leader must, therefore, take time for introspection to ensure that his motivation stays strong enough to motivate and inspire others.

If a leader really leads by example, then it is not necessary to threaten, blackmail, force or beg people to do their best. People will follow him voluntarily and will work hard in order to please him. It is therefore clear that the pastor, counsellor or member of the church council who is not himself motivated to deliver work of a high quality is not able to motivate and inspire others.

The Quality of Leadership

In any organization of at least a moderate size there are various levels of supervision. The first line of supervision is undertaken by supervisors and team leaders. Above them are junior managers, middle managers and senior managers. All of these managers have the function of supervision of one kind or another, although the supervisory tasks may differ in accordance with their level.

Churches and congregations usually have only two levels of authority, consisting of the church council and the rest of the congregation. In a church there is no place for a hierarchy with higher and lower ranks for believers; all members are, after all, equal and on the same footing, as we are all children of our Heavenly Father (Gal. 3: 26–28). Some of them are, however, called to be leaders and they receive certain gifts to perform their tasks.

Since the church is a voluntary organization (nobody can be forced to join a church or a congregation and nobody can be prevented from dissociating himself from a church or a congregation), it is inappropriate to try and organize it like a business. Businesses have hierarchies and people can be coerced to work in a certain manner and to maintain certain standards. In the church it may be expected of people to behave in a certain manner, but only because they are supposed to support and uphold certain doctrines, norms and principles from the Bible. Generally, people join a specific church because they agree with that church's approach, views and culture. Nobody in the church can be forced to behave in a certain manner – he may, however, be *motivated* to behave as an obedient believer.

Any good leader keeps his followers informed regarding plans and decisions. He also communicates his followers' problems and concerns to the appropriate entities in the organization. It has been found that if there is good communication between management and the workforce in an organization it will have a positive influence on job satisfaction and morale, leading to a lower turnover of personnel.

In the same manner it is important that church councils keep the members of the congregation informed about their plans, goals and decisions – as well as about their successes, failures, losses and gains, and changes regarding the policies and rules of the church. It is also important to make the circumstances of members known, so that prayers of request or thanksgiving can be said on their behalf.

Leadership is an art that may be taught. Not all leaders are natural leaders who can lead from the front through the force of their characters and personalities. Therefore, most good leaders need to be trained to perform their tasks effectively and sensitively. They must be trained to handle conflict in the church, to offer guidance to members and to provide counselling where needed.

Participative Leadership

Leaders can be either more or less authoritarian. The current trend is towards a participative style of leadership, which is more democratic. That means that decisions are explained to group members instead of being forced upon them, and that the group is even involved in the decision-making process. In a similar vein, the members of a congregation have to be consulted by their church council. There is a growing awareness that all members of a congregation can play a constructive role because all of them have received certain gifts. Such a strategy ensures that decisions of the church council are more easily accepted and that parish members get more involved in the goals and activities of the church.

Effective and democratic leaders – also in the church – have clear goals and they inspire their followers to participate in the attainment of those goals. They are, furthermore, sensitive to the welfare of their followers, are focused on quality and know how to utilize rewards in a wise manner. Good leaders have mastered the art of requesting so that it does not seem as if they as begging, pleading, threatening or demanding.

There are certain rules that democratic leaders can follow in order to perform their tasks effectively:

- Plan and apportion tasks effectively;
- Promote the development of members;
- Keep followers informed about all decisions;
- Provide reasons for all decisions or requests;
- Consult with members regarding matters affecting them;
- Respect the right to privacy and other human rights of members;
- Help members with their personal problems; and
- Represent the interests of members and the group/congregation in the outside world.

Moral Leadership

A good leader, in both an ecclesiastical and a secular setting, has to set an example of moral leadership. If the leader expects his followers to do the right thing, he has to lead by example.

How do we discern between right and wrong behavior? How do we evaluate the actions of people as good or bad? For a Christian, the answer is obvious: the route to moral and ethical behavior is sufficiently signposted in the Bible. The prophets, apostles and other biblical authors have given us ample indications of God's will regarding our conduct.

The Bible, however, is not our only source of knowledge regarding moral and ethical behavior. God has given every normal person a conscience with which he can discriminate between good and bad, right and wrong in a given situation. God has written his law on the heart of every human being (Rom 2: 14 & 15). Accordingly, there is a great measure of consensus between well-meaning people across the globe as to what constitutes ethical and unethical behavior. What follows may be seen as such a consensus:

Ethical behavior can be divided into two elements:

- The dichotomy or difference between right and wrong; and
- The dichotomy or difference between good and bad.

The first dichotomy rests on especially two values: responsibility and integrity. The second dichotomy also contains two important values: compassion and forgiveness or tolerance.[18]

Doing what is right means that we respect the law of God, the law of our country and the rights of others. The Bible praises the virtue of "righteousness" in many passages (Prov 12: 5 & 1 John 2: 29).

- *Responsibility* means that we must realize that we are responsible to God, to society and to ourselves. We must be able

---

[18] Lennick & Kiel, *Moral Intelligence,* passim.

to justify our decisions and actions as being the *right* decisions and the *right* actions (Matt 25: 31-46 & Acts 17:30). We must be able to "sell" our behavior to others and convince them that we did the right thing.

- *Integrity* means that we must be able to live with our own decisions and actions without violating our consciences. These decisions and actions have to accord with our principles and we need the strength of character to never deviate from our principles (Job 2: 3 & 2 Cor 7: 1-2). Doing what is good and fleeing from evil is summarized by Jesus' dictum: "Therefore, whatever you want men to do to you, do also to them, for this is the Law and the Prophets." (Matt 7: 12).
- *Compassion* involves charity, neighborly love and empathy with those experiencing misfortune, pain, heartache or tragedy. The Bible is full of injunctions for Christians to act with compassion, and Jesus was the supreme example of a man with compassion for others (Matt 9: 13; Matt 11: 28 – 30 & Col 3: 12).
- *Forgiveness* means that we act with tolerance towards those who have wronged us, because we understand that we are not perfect either. Jesus exhorted us to forgive each other seventy times seven (Matt 18: 21–22). We cannot expect God to forgive us our sins if we are not prepared to extend forgiveness towards others (Matt 6: 14–15).

The moral leader, therefore, has to be a leader with responsibility, integrity, compassion and forgiveness if he wishes to practice moral leadership.

Leadership Skills

People can be trained to be effective leaders. The idea that all good leaders are born leaders cannot be accepted anymore. There are certain skills that may be taught in order to help leaders to lead and manage more effectively:

Communication Skills

- Leaders need verbal communication skills. They must be able to give concise, clear and accurate explanations and requests, ask the right questions to gain information and to advise people so that they can perform their tasks. Good communication requires the following of the leader:
  o Communicating at the level of the person he is talking to;
  o Ensuring that the message is received correctly;
  o Making sure that the other person knows how and when he must react and report back;
  o Communicating clearly what has to be done, how it is to be done, how well it is to be done, when the task is to be completed and how to report back.
- Leaders need good non-verbal communication skills. They must have the right social attitudes, appropriate emotions, and assertiveness and must be presentable.

Other Necessary Skills

In addition to the above, participative leadership needs the following skills:

- The ability to lead a group to consensus;
- The ability to listen;
- The ability to delegate tasks;
- The ability to defuse conflict (more about this later on);
- The ability to provide feedback; and
- The ability to accurately evaluate the work and achievements of others (more about this later).

15. PLANNING, DECISION MAKING AND THE SOLUTION OF PROBLEMS

Read: John 4: 1–26

Discuss the conversation of Jesus with the Samaritan woman.

- *How did He treat her?*
- *What did the woman expect from the conversation?*
- *What did Jesus accomplish with the conversation?*

Read: Matt 6: 25–34; Matt 7: 24–28; Luk 14: 28–32

Discuss the following statement:

"It amounts to a lack of faith if you plan ahead. One must leave the future in the hands of God."

Read: James 4: 13–17

Which important principles must we keep in mind when planning our actions?

The Elements of Planning

It ought to be clear that no organization can survive without proper planning for the future. Any process of planning has to contain the following elements:

- *Estimating the future*: Nobody can predict the future with any certainty, but present trends may supply pointers for the days and years to come. The church has to be ready for new challenges and opportunities.
- *Establishing objectives*: Any organization must know where it is going and have clear goals. Every church must have clarity

about the question: what does God expect of us in the environment where we are living? What must we accomplish?

- *Developing policies*: The Word of God must be searched for principles that apply to the present situation with its challenges and opportunities.

- *Programming and establishing procedures*: There must be clarity about the methods to be utilized to reach the stated objectives. There must be a clear plan of action detailing what has to be done, when it has to be done, how well it has to be done, by whom it has to be done and how feedback on progress and obstacles have to be provided.

- *Budgeting*: If finances are needed for executing the plan of action, those finances have to be found and budgeted for.

There is no single fixed method for dealing with problems. Each situation needs its own approach. The following procedure, however, should deliver good results in most cases:

Identify the Problem

Before any problem can be solved, it is necessary to know exactly what the problem is.

It is, therefore, necessary to give the members of the meeting or the affected members ample opportunity to tell their whole story. Help them along by asking open questions and by concentrating initially on the emotional content of their story. After the story has been completed, a provisional conclusion about the nature of the problem can be reached. This conclusion may, of course, be revised during the course of the meeting or subsequent meetings.

Once the nature of the problem has been identified, it is also necessary to ask the following questions:

- How serious is the problem?

- When did it originate?
- What are the causes?
- What are the consequences?
- Who are the role players (if any)?

Identify the Desired Outcome

The next step is to identify the desired outcome, goal or end result. Ask those involved questions, such as these:

- What would you like to happen?
- How will you know when the problem is solved?
- What circumstances would make you feel happy/satisfied/good again?

Help the members to formulate their goals clearly. What this means is that if the goal has been reached, the problem ought to be solved.

Identify the Options

After the nature of the problem and the desired outcome have been determined, it is necessary to identify the various options open to the meeting or the stakeholders. This is a co-operative exercise. The members know their circumstances best and know which options exist as a possibility. The leader may also suggest various options from his own life experience. The meeting must then decide whether these options are viable or desirable.

All the options must be discussed thoroughly. The pros and cons of each should be identified, considered, and weighed up. The consequences of each option should be calculated and the reactions of all role-players considered. It may help to assign a weight to each pro and con – a point on a scale between 0 and 10. One may then add the points of each pro or con and decide whether there are more pros or cons attached to a certain option.

With this discussion in mind, the next step is to decide upon the best option.

Identify Resources

After the best option has been identified, a plan of action should be drawn up. Such a plan will be dependent upon the available resources.

Compile a list of all available resources, as well as all other resources that may be necessary for the attainment of the desired outcome. Resources include the following:

- Skills, talents, knowledge and opportunities available to the church or the people struggling with a problem;
- The people's or the church's strengths and good qualities;
- Available equipment and finances; and
- People with the needed skills, knowledge, and opportunities on who one could (possibly) rely.

It is moreover necessary to identify all possible obstacles and dangers, since they may get in the way of reaching the desired outcome.

The leader must guide the meeting with the necessary questions and suggestions in order to arrive at a comprehensive list of all necessary and available resources, as well as possible obstacles. If the problem is very serious, it may be necessary to call in the help of one or more experts or authorities: a psychologist, a medical practitioner, a social worker, an attorney, or a government department such as the Department of Labor, the police or the local magistrate's office.

Draw up a Plan

Once all the preliminary steps have been completed, a plan of action may be devised in order to reach a solution to the problem (Prov 21: 5). The inputs of as much people as possible who will be involved in the execution of the plan are necessary; people will only cooperate with a plan if they feel they share ownership of the plan. It is advisable to put the plan in writing as part of the minutes of the meeting. Such a plan must contain, amongst other things, the following:

- The desired outcome or goal;
- All actions needed to attain the desired outcome and to overcome all possible stumbling blocks;
- Deadlines for the completion of all the steps outlined in the plan;
- A description of the steps to be followed and naming those who are responsible for those steps;
- The identification of other role players/helpers and the contribution each one can make;
- A list of equipment, finances, skills and other resources needed;
- Interim goals that have to be reached on the way to the ultimate goal;
- Performance standards that have to be met since sloppy work and laziness won't lead to any worthwhile results; and
- Methods for reporting back to the meeting or the chairperson of the meeting to determine whether the plan is progressing satisfactorily.

Before the plan is finalized it would be good to consult other possible role players to find out whether they are available and, in a position, to contribute. Make sure that the plan does not contain any unethical or illegal steps, as that can only cause more problems.

The Meeting's Commitment

After a clear, detailed and practical plan has been put onto paper, the people involved or the meeting will most probably feel more in control of the situation. If the problem has been inspected from all angles, it is likely to seem less threatening and serious.

At this stage it is necessary to get the members' and other stakeholders' commitment that they will actually put the plan into practice. Ask them to make a firm promise in this regard and arrange for future opportunities to give a progress report, detailing any obstacles encountered and new opportunities to have emerged.

This commitment is important because no plan can work unless there is motivation to put it into operation. It is important that the execution of any plan should be monitored closely as unexpected problems and obstacles always occur and this may necessitate changes to the plan.

Plans in General

It is clear from the scriptural passages mentioned at the beginning of this chapter (Matt 6: 25–34; Matt 7: 24–28; Luk 14: 28–32) that one cannot get along in life without proper planning. It is also necessary for every church to plan ahead. The activities for every year have to be planned well before the start of the new year and they have to be approved by the church council and published in the form of an almanac or a newsletter. There have to be written plans and procedures for all the activities and eventualities in the life of the church.

The annual almanac may also be the way in which members are reminded of procedures to be followed in certain situations. Members have to know how the Sunday School operates, when the choir has its repetitions, when the church council and its committees have their meetings, what has to be done when couples wish to be married in church, how parents must go about when they want to have their infant baptized, how to communicate sickness, death and other important events to the pastor/priest/minister and how to organize a funeral. Rules for the renting of the church hall may be given on the almanac, together with the business hours of the administrative office of the church, how to make an appointment with the pastor/minister/priest and what the church's banking details are for those who wish to pay their tithes directly into the church's bank account.

16. MANAGING THE CULTURE OF A CHURCH

Read: 1 Cor 3: 1–4
How do you evaluate the culture of the church of Corinth?

When the word *culture* is mentioned most people tend to think of art forms such as music, architecture, sculpture, poetry etc. These forms of art certainly are aspects of the culture of a given society, but culture is actually a much wider concept. It has to do with all the values, traditions, beliefs and relationships prevalent in that society. These can be expressed by means of art, but they are more usually manifest in the life style and behavioral patterns of the people.

What follows is applicable to any organization – whether it is a commercial enterprise, a government department, a sports club or a church. All these types of organizations are comprised of people who fulfill different roles but who are also working together to achieve certain common goals.

Organizational Culture

All organizations (including churches) are characterized by their own different cultures. An *organization's culture* can be described as:

> the way things are being done by the members of that organization;

or –

> the values, goals, traditions, assumptions, beliefs, attitudes, rituals and relationships, which characterize that organization and help to establish its identity.

These values, goals, traditions, assumptions, beliefs, attitudes, rituals and relationships are usually taken for granted and are not always well articulated. They, nevertheless, exert a powerful influence over the actions of the members of the organization.

In a church it is supposed that these values, traditions, assumptions, beliefs, attitudes, rituals and relationships are governed by Biblical principles and precedents (Acts 20: 32, Eph 6: 17, 1 Thess 2: 13 & 2 Tim 3: 15).

The culture of an organization is transmitted and perpetuated by the example set by influential members of the organization. The way they usually do things and their comments on events set the trend and that is emulated by other members of the organization.

Every organization has, furthermore, certain stories, myths and legends about important events in the past. These stories explain the values of the organization and the way things are being done. The culture is usually initiated by the founders of the organization who deemed it necessary to do things in a certain manner and that sets the trend for the future.

In a large organization, subcultures are likely. Different departments or sections will have their own ways of doing things whereby their identity is highlighted.

Cultures may be strong or weak. In a small and young organization, it is to be expected that the members will not be as attached to the core values and traditions of the organization as in a large and older organization. The stronger and more entrenched a given culture is, the more stable it will be; efforts to change it will meet with resistance.

It is extremely difficult to merge two cultures. When one firm is taken over by another and their cultures are widely divergent then the merger will certainly cause much resentment and friction since people will not be very willing to adopt new values, strategies and relationships.

The same applies to churches. It happens that congregations have to merge, due to dwindling numbers of members, and this process has to be handled with great care. When two denominations decide to form one new denomination, it may lead to dissatisfaction by certain members and such a step have to be dealt with in such a manner that congregations preserve their identity as far as possible to prevent undue disruptions.

Cultural Dimensions

The culture of any enterprise or organization usually deals with the following issues:

- The identity of the organization;
- The organization's place in the world and its relationship with the environment;
- A frame of reference for interpreting events within and without the organization;
- The extent to which members of the organization identify with the organization as a whole and their loyalty towards it;
- The way members are treated, penalized and rewarded;
- The way clients and customers are treated;
- The importance given to the evaluation and assessment of the efforts of members;
- The importance given to the development and the careers of members;
- The way in which members who retire or quit are treated;
- The way decisions are made and how much decision-making authority and autonomy are given to juniors who are eager to be innovative and take the initiative;

- The extent to which supervisors, managers and leaders interfere with the work of their underlings or followers or give them support;
- How tight or how flexible the organizational structure is;
- The way in which risks and challenges are assessed and approached;
- The way in which the administration of the organization is handled; and
- Whether the organization sticks to its core business or ventures out into new fields.

The culture of any organization plays an important role in the day-to-day running of that organization. If leaders and other members have internalized the values and beliefs of the concern, they need less control since they can be counted upon to act and behave in a certain manner.

There is no question that the culture of some organizations is bad for productivity or the general health of the organization. If it is, for instance, acceptable that customers or outsiders are to be treated with disrespect, that the opinions of junior members count for nothing and that absolutely no risks are to be taken then it may be expected that productivity will be low or that the organizational health will be below standard.

A culture that is conducive to high productivity or creative action is a culture –

- That meets the ever-changing challenges of the external environment;
- That fits the organization's goals with the strategy of the organization; and
- That is aligned with the available technology.

It is necessary that management or the church council regularly conduct a cultural diagnosis in order to determine whether the current culture is appropriate.

Read: 1 Cor 1: 10–17 & 11: 20–22
What can we learn about the organizational culture of the church at Corinth?

Read: Rev 2: 18–29
What can we learn about the organizational culture of the church at Thyatira?

Read: Rev 3: 1–6
What can we learn about the organizational culture of the church at Sardis?

Pathological Cultures

An organization's culture may be seen as that organization's personality, just as every individual person also has his or her own personality.

A person is more than a conglomerate of body parts and organs. He or she is a unique entity and that unity and uniqueness is brought about by having a definite personality. Likewise, an organization as an entity is also more than the sum total of its constituent parts. This "more" comprises *inter alia* its culture – together with its structure, shape and internal relationships.

17. HEALTHY CHURCHES AND SICK CHURCHES

Every person has a number of personality flaws. We regard this as quite normal since no person is perfect. These flaws may, however, become pathological and that person may suffer from a personality disorder, a mood disorder, an anxiety disorder or a psychosis. In the same manner, organizations may also develop pathological personalities or cultures.

Researchers have identified the following types of pathological organizational cultures – which may also be true of certain churches or congregations:

- *The anti-social church:* This church has no respect for the rule of law and disregards the human rights of members.
- *The narcissistic church:* This church has an over-inflated view of its own importance and thinks that the rest of the world exists in order to serve its interests. It regards outsiders as an unavoidable evil that disturbs the church's peace.
- *The depressed church:* This type of church interprets events in the darkest colors possible. Everything is seen as a potential danger or calamity and absolutely no risks are taken.
- *The hyperactive church:* The members of this type of church are extremely busy. They have only one motivation for all their activities, and that is to impress the leader or the outside world – not to satisfy the clients of the church or to be loyal to Christ.
- *The compulsive church:* This type of church is unwilling to learn from its mistakes and keeps on repeating the same mistakes in a compulsive manner.

- *The schizophrenic church:* This church has lost touch with reality and creates its own reality. It doesn't try to ascertain what the members want or need and how technology has changed, but lives in its own world and stays busy with its own inner workings.
- *The paranoid church:* The prevalent culture in this type of church is that of distrust and suspicion. Everybody, including the church's own members, is suspected of plotting to harm the church.

It is almost unnecessary to say that churches with any of these cultures are doomed. These pathological cultures make their survival extremely unlikely – unless these cultures are changed.

Changing a Culture

If the church council is concerned about laziness and lack of commitment by the members and the negative influence of certain aspects of the organization's culture on organizational actions or organizational health then there are basically three strategies to follow:

- *The first option is to manage the existing culture and take advantage of the existing values and traditions.*

That means that management should know exactly which values and traditions are prevalent and which behaviors rest upon these values. This knowledge can only be acquired by being part of the organization for a certain length of time and having one's ear to the ground. The positive aspects of the culture must then be emphasized, encouraged and rewarded to such an extent that the less positive aspects become unimportant and eventually vanish.

The reverse can also be tried. Management could make it clear that certain attitudes and behaviors will be unacceptable in future. This has to be made part of the organization's ethical code and disciplinary policy. When people are caught in the act and found guilty in a fair hearing of transgressing the new values and norms certain sanctions may be imposed upon them.

It has to be stressed that churches are not in a position to punish members by withholding wages or imposing fines since they are voluntary organizations. It is, though, necessary to impose discipline according to the prescriptions of Jesus in Matt 18: 15 – 20.

This strategy must be applied with great circumspection because it may cause resentment and resistance. Punishing bad behavior must always be accompanied by rewarding good behavior.

- *The second strategy is to actively assist the socialization process of new members of the organization.*

New members have to be taught the ropes before they can start to operate independently and productively. It is easy for them to pick up bad habits when they have to observe bad examples most of the time. Sunday schools are the preferred tool in this regard for youngsters in a church. Often a mentor is assigned to a new adult member to help him or her to adjust to the new environment and to show him or her around. If this mentor can teach the new member the good values and beliefs of the organization's culture then the chances are that that person will be less likely to pick up bad habits.

- *The third option is to try and change the organization's culture and eliminate the less desirable elements thereof.*

This is easier said than done since cultures become deeply entrenched and resist change. The best way is to stage some sort of crisis. When an organization faces a crisis then change and adaptation is more likely. The crisis that is to be staged must be visible to all members. Such crises can be created by replacing the top echelon of the management team or by reorganizing and scrambling the structure of the organization. These crises will send out the message that things cannot continue along old paths and that a reappraisal of goals, strategies and methods is necessary. This must be accompanied by a well-publicized reformulation of the church's vision and mission.

Together with this, the church council ought to create new stories and myths by staging or organizing certain events, situations, rituals and incidents to illustrate the new values and beliefs. When an influential member of the organization, preferably the pastor, deliberately behaves counter to the existing culture it certainly will cause a stir. The story of the incident will be told and retold and when that member persists in behaving in that way a new tradition can be established. It is important not to inadvertently revert to the old ways because that will re-establish and strengthen the old culture.

Since cultures are resistant to change, it will not be an easy task to carry through. Organizations that change their culture usually need a minimum of two years to accomplish this. All the strategies mentioned above need to be implemented simultaneously and consistently in order to achieve results.

A church that succeeds in weeding out negative aspects of its culture and cultivating the more positive aspects will certainly succeed in improving the commitment of its members. These new positive aspects of the culture will prove to be just as resilient and enduring as the old negative aspects, which had to be changed with great difficulty.

Read: Rev 3: 7–13
What can we learn about the culture of the church at Philadelphia?

It is desirable that churches develop a culture –

- in which previously powerless members are empowered;
- of tolerance and mutual respect between the sexes and between members of different racial, cultural and language groups (Rom 12: 9 – 10 & 18 – 21);
- where there is a sensitivity for the needs and challenges of the external environment (Matt 9: 37 – 38);
- in which the satisfaction of the member is the first priority; and
- where superior performance, high productivity, loyalty and ethical behavior are held in high regard and receive recognition (Rom 12: 11).

Perhaps the easiest and most effective way of establishing a culture of performance in a church is to design an effective appraisal system. When members know that their performance and outputs are to be monitored, they are more likely to do their best and work efficiently and effectively. If the church council isn't interested in die performance and actions of members then these members will also show little interest in delivering good work or acting responsibly.

The topic of performance appraisal will be dealt with later.

18. INANCIAL MANAGEMENT IN THE CHURCH

Read: 2 Cor 8 & 9
What does Paul teach us here regarding the finances of the church?

Read: Mal 3: 10; 1 Cor 16: 1–4
How are churches to be financed?

Read: Acts 11: 27–30; I Cor 16: 3; 2 Cor 8: 19–21
Which sound principle of financial management do we find here?

Financial Obligations
No church can survive without money. Every congregation has financial responsibilities:

- The pastor/priest/minister has to receive a stipend to enable him to live;
- The church building and other properties have to be maintained and repaired;
- Insurance premiums have to be kept up-to-date;
- Municipal rates have to be paid;
- Charitable work has to be funded;
- Sister congregations in financial straits have to be aided;
- Missionaries have to be supported; and
- An administrative office has to be maintained.

Denominations as a whole also need money. They usually support –

- Seminaries or Bible Schools for the training of candidates to the ministry;
- Missionary work;
- Social workers;
- Charitable institutions, such as old age homes, orphanages and private Christian schools; and
- Administrative offices.

Funds for these institutions have to come from the various congregations.

Some authorities argue that a church has to spend more money on projects outside the borders of that church than it spends on itself. That is a laudable ideal. There are, however, many poor congregations, which cannot even support themselves and are dependent upon the help of neighboring congregations – as was the case with the church in Jerusalem in the time of the apostles. There are, though, churches that have huge incomes and the obligation rests upon them to use these funds to further the interests of the Kingdom of God and not to enrich themselves. The bad example of the church in Laodicea (Rev 3) serves as a warning in this regard.

Sources of Income
The only source of income for churches of which we read in the New Testament was voluntary donations or contributions by the members of the various churches.

Nowadays, other sources of income have also become available, but they should never be the main source of income:

- Dividends on investments;
- Interest on cash in the bank;
- Hiring out of the church hall for weddings and other functions;

- Providing catering services for weddings and other occasions; and

- Legacies (which are, strictly speaking, also voluntary donations).

Members of congregations cannot be forced to donate certain sums of money to the church. These donations are voluntary. They must, however, be seen as a sign of our gratitude towards God for his saving grace through Jesus Christ, who paid with his life so that we may be saved – as Paul eloquently explains in 2 Cor 8 and 9.

The Administration of Funds

There can be no doubt that the financial matters of a church have to be managed scrupulously. That money is, after all, trust money. It was donated by the members of the church for specific purposes and may only be used for those purposes (usually those listed above).

The final responsibility for the administration of finances rests with the church council. The day-to-day administration of these funds must be entrusted to a treasurer who must be somebody who knows how to keep adequate financial records. That treasurer may be a full-time job in the administrative office of the church or may be a part-time and voluntary position. It is a good idea that his treasurer be supported by a financial committee of the church council.

It is a sound principle that more than one person has to sign cheques or have to be involved with the electronic transfer of funds – a principle that Paul advocated. This prevents dishonesty or an accusation of impropriety.

It goes without saying that the administration of the finances of a church have to comply with all legal requirements, guidelines given by the denomination, the requirements set by banks and other financial institutions and accepted practices regarding financial management. That includes the drawing up of an annual budget, which has to be approved by the church council and communicated to the congregation.

It has already been argued that the church cannot operate without plans. The annual budget is nothing but a financial plan. It stipulates how much income is expected and how much has to be spent on a number of projects during the next financial year. It ought to be standard practice that no expenditures shall be made, except those specified in the budget, although a contingency fund may be kept for unexpected urgent expenditures.

It has to be noted that the most important of these principles are also to be found in the Bible, as noted at the beginning of this chapter.

Responsibility Towards the Members of the Church

It has already been stated that the church is not a secret organization and that there has to be total transparency regarding all its actions – including the management of finances. For that reason, it is incumbent that the financial books and records of the church be audited annually and that the financial documentation be open for inspection by any member of the congregation.

Since the church council is, in last resort, responsible for the management of the church's money matters, a financial report has to be presented at each meeting. This report has to give the figures for income and expenditure and these figures have to be compared with the budget. The financial report also has to state which financial obligations and liabilities the church has, as well as the value of its assets.

The annual financial report of the church, including the budget, has to be available to the whole congregation and a special meeting of the congregation may even be called to explain this report. This report may be distributed by means of electronic mail or the church's newsletter to all members of the congregation.

19. CHURCH ARCHIVES

Read: Luk 1: 1–4

How did the author of the Gospel of Luke manage to gather the material for his story? Did he have any written records to rely on?

Read: Acts 15: 23–29

How did it happen that this resolution of the meeting in Jerusalem, quoted in this passage, was preserved and included in the book of Acts?

Every organization produces lots of paper work and that also applies to the church. That implies that a proper filing system has to be in place into which documents can be sorted according to type: invoices, correspondence with other churches, correspondence with the local authorities, correspondence with members of the congregation, bank statements, *etcetera*.

The following types of documentation have, in addition, to be created and stored in a safe place:

- A membership register in which all new and departing members are noted (often with their contact details);
- A register of all baptisms;
- Minutes of meetings of the church council and all its committees;
- Minutes of meetings of superior bodies, such as circuits, councils, classes, synods, general meetings *etcetera*;
- Newsletters and notices to the congregation (make print-outs of e-mail newsletters and letters);

- A book in which the accrued leave of absence for all paid employees is recorded and calculated according to their contracts of service;
- Financial records, including all invoices, proof of payments, receipts, bank statements, financial reports, budgets and auditors' reports.

In our digital age much correspondence and other forms of communication is being done via electronic mail. Documents stored on the hard drive of a computer are easily accessible, but this is not a very secure method of storage. Computers sometimes contract viruses or simply crash and then their memories are gone. It is recommended that print-outs of all documentation on good quality paper be kept for future reference and that back-ups of the contents of the memories of all computers be made regularly.

Many denominations require from their congregations to submit copies of registers to a central archive and to store all outdated correspondence, minutes and other documentation with this archive, where they are accessible to historians and others.

It is always good for any organization to leave a paper trail regarding all actions, transactions and dealings in order to prevent any misunderstandings in future, as well as having all the facts ready whenever a dispute of whatever sort arises.

20. COMMUNICATION AND MARKETING

Read: Acts 14: 27; 15: 30–33.

- _Would you agree that the church may be regarded as a secret association? Motivate your answer._
- _What role does communication play in the church?_

The Functions of Communication

It can be safely stated that the business of the church can be summarized in one word: communication. Christianity would never have been able to become the strongest and biggest religion in the world if it did not communicate its history, principles and faith across the world. After all, the whole Bible is a complex instrument of communication in which prophets, poets, apostles, historians and teachers of wisdom communicated their faith, knowledge and insights to their followers and the rest of humanity.

The minister/priest/pastor is the most important communicator in a church and all his tasks amount to some or other form of communication. [19] He is also the focal point of all lines of communication inside the congregation. He, therefore, fulfils a central role.

No organization can exist without information and communication channels. This is especially true of the church since one of the most important tasks/activities in the church is the dissemination of the message of the Gospel. She must communicate her policies and beliefs, comment on important events and how they are to be interpreted and inform people about church activities. The

---

[19] Heyns and Pieterse, _Eerste Treë_, 49–52.

success of an organization depends largely on the quality of its information.[20]

The goal of internal information within an organization amounts to the following:

- It creates a common purpose and goal or focus for all its members;
- It co-ordinates the tasks of all holders of official positions;
- It is necessary for making decisions; and
- It creates mutual respect and trust between the members and strengthens their morale and motivation.[21]

There are two types of information channels within any organization: formal and informal. Informal information channels are usually faster than the formal channels and are comprised of networks of friends, gossip and the grapevine. It is, though, less accurate that formal channels that rely on the written word and official meetings.[22]

This also applies to a congregation. The pastor/priest/ minister is the most important communicator and all his tasks (preaching, teaching, praying, administering the sacraments, pastoral care, administration *etcetera*) amount to some or other type of communication, whether oral, written or by means of his actions and example.[23] He is also the centre of all the communication lines within the congregation. He plays, therefore, a key role. It often happens, though, that the minister/pastor/priest is the last person to hear of problems. He also seldom receives feedback regarding the

---

[20] Tosi *et al.*, *Managing Organizational Behavior,* 447.

[21] Tosi et al., *Managing Organizational Behavior,* 447.

[22] Tosi *et al*, *Managing Organizational Behavior,*448.

[23] Heyns and Pieterse, *Eerste Treë,* 49–52)

quality of his performance. It goes without saying that if he is not well informed about what is happening in his church, he cannot do a good job.

Information Channels

The structure of an organization has an influence on the effectiveness and quality of the communication. The following factors play a role:

- Communication between people of widely different status is more difficult than communication between people on the same level;
- Communication from the bottom upwards is usually less efficient than otherwise. Management often hears of grievances or problems on grass roots level when it is too late to do something. Feedback from the lower levels can, therefore, be a problem;
- A complex system with many subsystems complicates the communication process since more channels have to be created;
- Communication is easier when the people affected perceive it to be in their interest;
- Communication flows more easily if there are more direct channels from the centre to the periphery and between subsystems;
- It helps when members belong to more than one subgroup; a member of the church council may, for instance, also be a Sunday school teacher or sing in the choir and be the leader of a Bible study group; this type of situation creates informal links between the subgroups and stimulates the flow of information.

- If there are too many links in the communication process it can lead to blockages and distortions of the message.[24]
- Differences in gender and culture make communication more difficult since it may lead to misunderstanding.[25]

Every organization creates its own culture – consisting of traditions, values, perceptions, attitudes and procedures which are being shared by all or most members. This determines the character or personality of the organization. It plays an important role in the continued existence of the organization by being a binding factor between the members by strengthening their loyalty and motivation. People identify themselves with an organization when they approve of its culture and when the members trust and support each other.[26]

The culture of a congregation is largely dependent upon the input of the pastor. He is, after all, the most important communicator in the congregation and his ideas, preferences, style of ministry and values have, inevitably, a large influence on the members.

It is important for every church to employ every available channel of communication. In previous centuries, churches communicated mostly by means of the spoken word during church services, meetings and person-to-person conversations. The written word was also employed in books, pamphlets and periodicals. In our time, there are many more opportunities due to the electronic revolution that hit our world. It is fairly easy to do desk-top publishing in the administrative office of a church to produce printed newsletters. Churches may also communicate through the radio,

---

[24] Tosi *et al.*, *Managing Organizational Behavior,* 448, 462–66.

[25] Tosi *et al.*, *Managing Organizational Behavior,* 456, 457.

[26] Meares, Á Model for Changing", 38; Tosi *et al.*, *Managing Organizational Behavior,* 741.

television, websites, electronic mail to members, text messages on mobile phones and other social media.

If the church neglects these opportunities the danger exists that the voice of the church will be drowned out by all the other secular media, each with its own message and appeal. It is important for every congregation to have a clear communication strategy, approved by the church council. Every church must realise that it has a most valuable product to offer to the market – the Gospel of Jesus Christ. This marketing drive can only work if the church demonstrates to the world that this message lives in the hearts and minds of its members.

All these channels amount to top-down communication. It is also very important that the governing body of a church be aware of everything that goes on within the church and that bottom-top communication also takes place. Nowadays, it is very easy for parishioners to contact their minister/pastor/priest by telephone, text messages or e-mail to inform him of sickness, death or other emergencies. In many churches, every member of the church council has his own ward to care for and news about important developments in every household in these wards can easily be passed on to those who have to deal with them.

Church councils also have to encourage the informal dissemination of information by creating opportunities for members to get together in various configurations: Bible study groups, care groups, house churches, prayer meetings, outings by certain groups, *etcetera*.

21. MANAGING THE EDUCATIONAL TASK OF THE CHURCH

Read: Deut 4: 9; Deut 6: 6–7; 2 Tim 3: 15
What are the duties of parents towards their children?

When Jesus was ministering in Galilee, Judea and Jerusalem, he was regarded as a wise teacher and people often addressed Him as "Rabbi". He taught his disciples (the word "disciple" means pupil or apprentice) how to perform their ministries and he even gave them practice by sending them out to proclaim his message on their own.

All the books of the Bible have an educational goal; they were written to instruct the people of God about God, his will for mankind, how his people are to worship Him and how to behave towards their fellow human beings. It must be stressed: the church has a definitive educational role to play towards its members and even towards the world in general.

Education at Home
God expects of each family to be a miniature church where the parents instruct their children in the Bible and the Christian faith (Deut 4: 9; Deut 6: 6–7; Josh 24: 15; Eph 6: 4). Parents must frequently be reminded of this task.

Sunday Schools
It is hard to imagine a church without a Sunday school. The children of today are the adult members of the church of tomorrow and they ought to be instructed in our Christian faith, the contents of the Bible and a Christian way of living.

Of course, this activity has to be managed well; otherwise, the time of everybody will be wasted. Sunday school teachers are all volunteers, but it may be necessary to give them some training. Good reading material must be provided to the children; fortunately, most denominations make provision for this.

Training for Members of the Church Council and Others

The church's educational role does not end with Sunday Schools and the instruction of children by their parents. Adult members also need ongoing training.

Members of the church council – especially new members – need some training as to how to perform their tasks. Some church councils have ongoing training as a fixed item on the agendas of all their meetings, but it may also be necessary to schedule special occasions with this purpose.

All Christians will profit from courses on topics like effective parenthood, witnessing in the world, better marriages and pastoral care and counselling. Many churches run a Bible school for their members in which they can follow a basic course in theology and a certificate can be earned after a year or two.

It may be assumed that most members of a church have certain talents and spiritual gifts. These talents and gifts have to be identified and developed so that more and more believers may become involved in the running and operational aspects of the life of the church. If the church is to operate as the body of Christ, then the maximum number of members should become actively involved and be equipped to perform the tasks for which they have received talents and gifts.

This all means that every church should be serious about its educational task and see to it that this is organized properly.

22. MANAGING THE CHARITABLE TASK OF THE CHURCH

Read: Luk 10: 29–37

- *What can we learn from this parable regarding the calling of Christians?*
- *Do you know who your neighbor is?*

Read: Acts 4: 32–35

Can we follow the example of the church in Jerusalem in all respects?

The charitable task of the church can be executed in an informal and spontaneous way – as the Good Samaritan did – or it may be an organized activity that is managed by the church council.

Spontaneous and Informal Charity

Jesus had a soft heart for poor people, the downtrodden, the lonely and the sick. The Gospels contain many reports of how He fed people, how He gave attention to women and children, how He visited the lonely (Saggaeus!) and how He healed people with all sorts of afflictions. Christians, who have Christ in their hearts, are supposed to follow his example.

In his parable of the sheep and the goats, Jesus made it clear that when we feed the hungry, clothe the naked, give something to drink to the thirsty, house the homeless, nurse the sick and visit those who are unjustly imprisoned, we are actually doing it to Him (Matt 25: 31–46).

All this means that all Christians are called upon to help others who are in need of assistance.

Formal Charity by the Church

The charitable work of the church is usually seen as a part of the tasks of deacons. We read in Rom 16: 1-2 of Phoebe, a deaconess of the church in Cenchreae (a suburb of Corinth), who was in charge of housing visiting Christians and who also provided lodgings to Paul.

It has been mentioned previously that no church can survive without decent planning. The annual budget is part of this planning. In the annual budget, funds have to be allocated to the charitable work of each church.

It is to be recommended that each church draw up contingency plans and procedures for all types of eventualities. The following types of crises come to mind:

- Members of the church who have lost their jobs and their income have to be supported;
- Emotional and material support to be provided to people who are in mourning;
- Catering to be done for funeral guests;
- The sick to be visited and even nursed;
- Victims of crime and violence to be helped to get over the trauma;
- Drug addicts and alcoholics who struggle to get out of the grip of their chemical dependency are to be helped to go for rehabilitation;
- Mothers and their children who have to flee from abusive husbands/partners and fathers and have to be given a temporary safe haven until they can find alternative lodgings; and
- The elderly and the lonely who need social support.

These plans ought to be in writing, have to be updated at regular intervals and be readily available when needed.

The pastor/minister/priest of the church is as a matter of course involved in all these tasks. He is, after all, supposed to be trained as a pastoral counsellor. But he cannot do everything and he needs volunteers who are able to help with these cases on an ongoing basis.

Many denominations employ social workers to help churches to deal with the worst cases. It is also important for churches to refer people to professionals when they encounter serious problems, such as lawyers, social workers, psychologists or medical practitioners. Some denominations provide social services by having established old aged homes, children's homes, safe homes for abused women and children, rehabilitation centers of people with chemical dependency and schools for children with special needs. The state subsidies for these establishments are usually not enough to cover all the costs and aid from the churches is also needed.

23. MANAGING THE PROPHETIC TASK OF THE CHURCH

Read: Acts 1: 8
What was the last request that Jesus gave to his disciples?

Read: 1 Pet 5: 1–4
What are the tasks of elders in the congregation?

The Informal Prophetic Task

Jesus Christ was anointed by the Holy Spirit when he was baptized by John the Baptist to become our King, High Priest and Prophet (Matt 3: 16). All Christians, who belong to Jesus Christ, also have this threefold anointing. We are all, therefore, supposed to be also prophets and explain God's message to our neighborhood and environment.

Unfortunately, many Christians do not quite know how to be efficient and effective witnesses for Christ. They know that Jesus sent his followers out in the world to make disciples (Matt 28: 19), but they are at a loss how to do that.

There are various courses in spiritual counselling available to train people in this regard. The church council of every church ought to organize events where members of the congregation can be trained to become effective evangelists.

The Formal Prophetic Task

The minister/priest/pastor of each congregation is trained to perform this prophetic task. The elders of the congregation have the task of oversight or supervision – also regarding the messages brought from the pulpit. They must guard against any unbiblical ideas or heresies dished up to the congregation.

It is a good idea if the priest/pastor/minister regularly asks some elders – three or four – to evaluate his sermons. A short form on which a score out of 10 may be given and which contains the following items may be handed out:

Evaluation of Today's Sermon

Today's date: ………………………………………………………………..
Scripture reading: ………………………………………………………..
Please give a point out of 10 for each of the following items or provide the required information:

- How well was the sermon prepared?
………………………………………………………………………..

- How well were you able to understand the central message?
………………………………………………………………………..

- Did you receive new insights into the Word of God? [Yes/No]
- How well did the sermon explain the Word of God?
………………………………………………………………………..

- Did the sermon provide enough background information about the text that was being explained?
………………………………………………………………………..

- How well did the sermon shed light on the current situation in the church and elsewhere?
………………………………………………………………………..

- Was there anything in the sermon you don't agree with? Please provide details:
………………………………………………………………………..

- What did you enjoy most about the sermon?
………………………………………………………………………..

These forms may be discussed afterwards with the persons who completed them. That will certainly help the preacher to know how well his sermons are getting through to the congregation and how he may, perhaps, improve his preparation.

24. MOTIVATING AND MOBILIZING MEMBERS

Read: 2 Cor 5: 14–15
What motivated Paul to endure hardship?

What is Motivation?

Motives play a decisive role in human behavior. For every action there is some or other motive and that flows from the fact that people are free and responsible creatures who make choices and decisions and may be held accountable for their choices and decisions.

Motivation may be described as –

> those factors that determine or regulate behavior. This implies that behavior is being caused by the person himself and that it is directed by determinants such as motives, needs, drives and goals. Motivation is therefore to be distinguished from other determinants of behavior such as abilities and external stimuli from the environment.

Motivation stems from two sources: from within and from outside. Psychologists distinguish between intrinsic motivation and extrinsic motivation.

Intrinsic motivation is essentially self-motivation. It flows from internal factors such as a person's attitude towards his work and life in general, his interests, value system, ideals, beliefs, feelings, self-confidence, self-concept and willpower.

Extrinsic motivation is essentially the application of incentives and external determinants of behavior by an agency other than the person himself. Under these the following may be counted:

the provision of ways and means for the fulfillment of biological, psychological and spiritual needs, methods applied to coerce or force somebody into compliance, punishment and rewards.

Human beings, like all life forms, have certain needs that have to be satisfied for them to survive. These needs can be divided into physical or biological needs, psychological needs and spiritual needs. These needs serve as motivators and determinants of human behavior. If a person has some or other need that has to be satisfied, he is moved to do something about the matter.

One reason why Christianity has survived so long is that it managed to satisfy some or most of the human needs of its adherents. A short description of these various needs is necessary before it can be explained how the church may be able to satisfy these needs and, thereby, motivate its members to become active and enthusiastic participants of the life and work of the church.

It has to be added that no church can force its members to behave in a certain way. Nor can any church punish its members. They can only be motivated by a good example from the pastor and the church council, by appealing to their consciences and by satisfying their various needs.

Physical Needs

Physical or biological needs are obviously the need for nourishment, water, sleep and rest, oxygen, protection against the elements, warmth and movement or exercise. Nobody can stay alive if these needs are not satisfied.

Psychological Needs

There is no consensus among psychologists with regards to the nature of the psychological needs of humans. The categorization that follows, however, seems to be useful.

One can deem psychological needs to include the following (in order of importance): the need for identity, the need for stimulation and the need for security. Many people would like to add the need for love; that may, however, be seen as a combination of all three above-mentioned needs.[27] These needs have to be explained in more detail:

The Need for Identity

The need for identity means that every human being would like to be recognized as an individual, as a unique person with human dignity. He needs to receive recognition for work well done, to be regarded highly and to be respected by others.

His identity is largely dependent upon the people and groups to which he belongs: life partner, family, circle of friends, group of colleagues, church and neighborhood. With these people and within these groups he has a certain status and performs a certain role.

A person's identity is coupled with his address: the piece of the earth that he calls home. People who do not have a property of their own find it difficult to settle down. Who wants to be bound to an apartment on the tenth floor?

Identity is determined by a person's history, his *past*, the road along which he has travelled to reach the present and the factors in his past that made him the person he has become.

The Need for Stimulation

The need for stimulation arises from the way the human brain is hard-wired. We all avoid boredom and a shortage of stimulation like the plague. This is why life is so difficult for elderly people, invalids and patients; they have nothing to occupy themselves with.

---

[27] Ardrey, *The Territorial Imperative* 358–70.

People will even suppress their need for security in favor of stimulation. That is why so many people exchange a somewhat safe existence in rural areas for the excitement of city lights and squatter camps. People engage in certain relationships – even dangerous ones – on account of the excitement they experience, even though this may endanger their safe relationships.

Love between people of the opposite sexes wanes when excitement and stimulation disappear from the relationship.

The need for stimulation and excitement is concerned with the *present*. People want to make the most of the moment in which they are living, including having religious experiences.

The Need for Security

The human need for security is fairly obvious. It is reassuring to know where one stands with people, especially with a life partner. A person may toil at a tedious job for many years, as it holds out the promise of a secure existence. A person's address also gives security; if there is a "place under the sun" he can call his own he more readily feels safe and secure, and he will – if needs be – fight to keep it his own.

This need is focused on the *future*. People dislike unpleasant surprises and they need to know what they can expect from tomorrow and next year.

The need for security often clashes with the need for stimulation. This may be the source of much stress and conflict.

Spiritual Needs

The highest needs of a human being – his spiritual needs – are his needs for meaning in life and for freedom and responsibility.

It is important for every person to experience that life makes sense. Viktor Frankl has demonstrated very convincingly that people are prepared to endure extreme difficulties and hardship as long as it makes sense.[28] Rossouw declares that the question regarding the meaning of life is "the most critical question" that anyone can pose. This question deals with "the humanity of man", and when he seeks an answer without success, he "arrives at an existential crisis."[29]

It is a fact that a great deal of the suffering that people have to endure appears to them to be meaningless. Christians are convinced that life and everything connected to it only makes sense if they can experience it in relationship with God.

A sane human being is able to make decisions freely. Accordingly, he also has the need to put this freedom into practice. This need means that he seeks to have control over his own life. If he gets caught up in circumstances where this control becomes impossible, then the result is frustration and a feeling of powerlessness.

The down-side of human freedom is responsibility. One must always be able to justify one's decisions towards society and in the light of his own ethical principles. A normal human being is endowed with a conscience and it is unpleasant to be plagued by a bad conscience. Therefore, people find it best to practice their freedom of choice in a responsible manner.

Satisfaction of Human Needs by the Church

A very important reason why Christianity has survived through the ages is the fact that it was able to satisfy most or all of the psychological and spiritual human needs.

---

[28] Frankl, *The Will to Meaning,* 6.

[29] Rossouw, *Die Sin van die Lewe,* 6.

It can be said that a religious faith and affiliation fulfill the following three functions: it helps the believer –

- to discover meaning in life;
- to live according to moral norms and standards; and
- to receive social support.[30]

Shermer puts it this way:

> "Religion is a social institution that evolved to reinforce group cohesion and moral behaviour. It is an integral mechanism of human culture to encourage altruism.... and to reveal the level of commitment to cooperate and reciprocate among members of a social community. Believing in God provides an explanation for our universe, our world, and ourselves; it explains where we came from, why we are here, and where we are going. God is also the ultimate enforcer of the rules, the final arbiter of moral dilemmas, and the pinnacle object of commitment."[31]

It has already been argued that human beings seek meaning in life. Christianity usually provides in this need by pointing out that we were created by God to glorify him and to further the interests of his kingdom. Churches do this by means of sermons, Bible study groups, pamphlets, magazine articles, religious programmes on radio and television and religious books that explain the message of the Bible and the doctrines of the church.

---

[30] Louw, *Pastoraat en Ontmoeting,* 66; Meadow and Kahoe, *Psychology of Religion* 5.

[31] Shermer, *The Believing Brain,* 186.

Our faith also provides norms and standards for good and right behaviour. In the Bible, one finds, for instance, the Ten Commandments with certain prescriptions for good and moral behaviour. This provides in the need for freedom and responsibility. People are challenged to make certain decisions or choices and they have to respond to the dictates of their consciences.

Religious communities are usually geared to provide social support for those in need. There are usually mechanisms for helping the destitute, the poor, the grieving and the lonely. The human physical and psychological needs are, therefore, taken care of.

The need for identity is satisfied within a religious community. The individual feels part of a group and experiences himself as a child of God. He often gets recognition for a job well done. Especially charismatic groups provide in the need for stimulation and excitement with their ecstatic singing, speaking in tongues, dancing and rituals such as healing or exorcism. The need for security is satisfied when a believer is reassured that he is a child of God, that his eternal fate in heaven is guaranteed and that he can rely on the support of other members of the group when experiencing distress.

The way to motivate members of the congregation is, therefore, to provide as far as possible in their human needs, be they physical, psychological or spiritual.

It is necessary that members be motivated to participate in the life of the church. The church is, after all, the body of Christ. We are his hands, feet, eyes, ears, mouth and heart and we are called upon to continue the ministry that Jesus started when he was on earth. This can only be the case where people are inspired to live as Christians and to follow Christ.

25.   MANAGING CHANGE

Read: Matt 21: 12–16
What type of change did Jesus try to bring about?

It is necessary that reformation and revival take place in the church on a regular basis. No church or congregation can ever be satisfied with its mistakes and failings and improvement must be constantly sought.

We must also be aware of the fact that we are living in a fast-changing world. The world during the second and third decades of the twenty-first century is very different from the world of twenty or thirty years ago. And we can be very certain that the world will be very different in the not too far off future. Churches have to be ready to face new challenges and needs in the time to come. This means that the church must constantly reinvent herself – which boils down to a continuous process of reformation and revival.

It is, therefore, necessary to deal with the subjects of reformation and revival – from a biblical perspective, but also from the insights of organizational psychology. It has to be emphasized in the first place that reformation and revival are not the same process, although there is a close connection between the two. Reformation means that the church gets rid of heresies and sinful practices, while revival is needed to heal a sick and dying church to be ready for new challenges.

Reformation
The Bible teaches us much about reformation. In brief, it means that no church is supposed to be satisfied with itself and with malpractices in its midst. Self-investigation has to be conducted

regularly. In the Old Testament one finds the following examples where the people of Israel, the faith community of that time, had to be reformed:

- We are informed in 2 Chr 19 that king Jehoshaphat of Judah reformed the chaotic judicial system of the country and appointed new judges. His goal was to reform the judicial system in accordance with the laws of God.

- We read in 2 Kings 22 and 23 of a reformation in the time of king Josiah of Judah. The high priest informed the king that he discovered the book of laws of the Lord in a store room in the temple complex. It was most probably the book of Deuteronomy that got lost in the meantime. The king ordered that the whole book be read to him. When he heard what God expected from his people, he rented his garments and acknowledged that his people got lost on a wrong track. He then ordered that all idolatry be removed from the country and that the people obey the laws of God.

- In the time of Ezra and Nehemiah something similar happened. Chapter 10 of the book of Ezra relates that many Jews who returned to the country of Judea after the Exile had married pagan women. Ezra managed to convince the priests and other leaders that this was a mistake and the ordered these men to send their pagan wives away. There were even priests who were married to foreign women. This was a reformation, the abolishing of wrong practices.

- We are informed in Nehemiah 13 that Nehemiah, the governor of Judah, convened a meeting of all Jews in Jerusalem. The law of God was read in the presence of all and on account of that a number of reforms were instituted.

In other words, reformation means to turn back from a wrong track and to become obedient to the Word of God (again).

There are no direct examples in the New Testament where reforms took place. We must remember that the history of the church in the New Testament spans merely a few decades, while the history of the Old Testament describes the events of a few centuries. We do read, however, of churches that went astray and where a reformation became necessary.

- In his two letters to the church at Corinth the apostle Paul mentions a number of issues which had to be rectified. There was disunity and a lack of unanimity. Some people abused the Lord's Supper to become drunk. There were Christians who practiced immorality. These matters had to be addressed and a reformation was necessary in the Corinthian church.

- In the letter to the church of Thyatira in Rev 2 the members are admonished for the fact that they allowed a false prophetess with the nickname of Jezebel to lead them astray. John, the author, predicted that the Lord would punish her with a sickbed. On the other hand, he also complimented those in that church who stayed faithful to the Word of God.

- In the letter to the church at Pergamum – also in Rev 2 – the congregation is warned not to accept the teachings of the so-called Nicolaitans and to convert themselves.

It was one of the slogans of the great Reformation during the sixteenth century: *Ecclesia reformata semper reformanda*. It is Latin and it means: the reformed church must constantly be reformed.

It was certainly necessary that a reformation took place in those days because there many malpractices and superstitions in the church of that time. The Lord called a man such as Martin Luther to start a reformation. That led to a schism in the Roman Catholic

Church of those days and a large part of Christianity became Protestant.

In the meantime, the Roman Catholic Church itself acknowledged that there were many malpractices in those days that needed rectification. It has to be pointed out that the last three popes, the spiritual leaders of the Roman Catholic Church, more than once asked forgiveness for the fact that pedophile priests were protected in the past. These priests are now being disciplined and even defrocked. This is also an example of a reform.

Revival

Revival is necessary when a church becomes sick or is dying. In the letter to the church at Sardis (Rev 3: 2 – 3) we read:

> "Be on the watch, and make strong the rest of the things which are near to death; because as judged by me your works have not come up to God's measure. Keep in mind, then, the teaching which was given to you, and be ruled by it and have a change of heart. If then you do not keep watch, I will come like a thief, and you will have no knowledge of the hour when I will come on you."

We also get this advice for a sick church in James 5:16 –

> "So then, make a statement of your sins to one another, and say prayers for one another so that you may be made well."

In other words: prayer and confession of sins are necessary conditions for a healthy and revived church.

We must also keep in mind that conversion is something that has to be repeated on a daily basis. There is, of course, an initial conversion when one meets the Lord for the first time. But then one must convert every single day after that because there always remain ugly and bad habits and practices in one's life. Jesus taught us in the Lord's Prayer to pray every day that God will forgive us our sins; that means that we have to investigate our lives every day and get rid of bad habits with the help of God. Paul writes in Rom 6: 13 to the Christians in Rome –

> "And do not give your bodies to sin as the instruments of wrongdoing, but give yourselves to God, as those who are living from the dead, and your bodies as instruments of righteousness to God."

This instruction is not only applicable to the individual believers – it also has to apply to every congregation and the church as a whole.

Organizational Psychology

We can also learn much from organizational psychology in this regard.

In a previous chapter, various types of sick churches were listed. It is necessary to have a look at the warning signs, symptoms and stages of disintegration of these sick churches – churches that can only be revived through a thorough process of reformation and revival.

There are various *warning signs* that herald the death of any organization, the church included. The most important warning signs are the following:

- *Arrogance and megalomania:* If a church is convinced that it has the full truth and that it never makes mistakes, the end may be near. It forgot the adage that pride comes before the fall.

- *Tolerance for incompetence:* When laziness, sloppy work and incompetence are tolerated, the writing is on the wall for that church.
- *Lack of strategic targets:* A healthy church knows where it is going, what its long-term goals are and how to reach them. The church that just stumbles along each day and each year without looking ahead and is only interested in its own survival is doomed.
- *Lack of effective communication:* When church members do not know what is going on in their church they easily leave for another church where communication is better.
- *Seeking culprits:* The sick church tends to blame all its ills on external factors without looking at its own shortcomings.
- *Resistance to change:* The status quo is all important for the sick church; any form of change seems to be dangerous.

The sick and dying church shows the following *symptoms* that are characteristic of a dying organization:

- *Infighting:* There are increasingly internal tensions because everybody still wants his slice of a diminishing cake. Factions and parties are formed and they combat each other.
- *Increasing conflict and intrigues:* If members of a church start plotting against each other in an endeavour to gain positions of influence, that church is surely dying. These factions endeavour to minimise the influence of the other and they blame each other for the setbacks suffered.
- *Leaders lose credibility:* When the pastor and members of the church council are at each other's throats their credibility, inevitably, suffers.
- *Increasing turnover of volunteers:* The groups within the sick church depend on volunteers to perform certain tasks. When

these volunteers do not feel at home any more in this sick organization they just disappear and it is not always easy to find replacements.

- *Decreased motivation of members:* The members of a dying organization usually lose their loyalty and interest in that organization. Their willingness to contribute their time, energy, expertise and money disappears.
- *Unethical behaviour:* Organizations that are on their way out often rely on unethical actions in an endeavour to survive. This cannot work because these actions cannot stay secret in the long run.

When all these warning signs and symptoms appear, it is inevitable that that church is on its way out. According to researchers, dying organizations progress through five *stages of decay*:

- *Denial:* The leaders of the sick church are blind to the process of decay and deny that anything is amiss; they ignore all the warning signs and refuse to look critically at their own actions.
- *Paralysis:* Due to all the infighting it is impossible to concentrate on the real reason for the existence of the church, namely to serve the interests of the Kingdom of God. In other words: the sick church becomes paralysed and inactive.
- *Panic:* When it dawns upon the leadership in the sick church that their church is dying, they easily go into a state of panic, unable to do something constructive and unable to work on a strategy to revive the church.
- *The crisis stage:* When the leadership of the church becomes paralysed and fall into a state of panic, it is very easy to slip into the next stage, the crisis stage. At this stage, it becomes increasingly clear that the church is doomed to become extinct. There are few members left, nobody volunteers to perform

essential tasks and the finances of the church are in a perilous state. Only a wholescale programme of reform and revival may revitalise this church and it might entail the removal of the whole leadership structure – the priest/minister/pastor included.

- *Disintegration:* If no programme of reform and revival gets off the ground that church is doomed and, in the end, she shuts her doors.

A program of reformation and revival in the church amounts to a complete change of culture in that church. The culture of an organization consists of the traditions, procedures, methods, values, goals, channels of communication and division of roles in that organization. These aspects develop over time and get fixed into rules and traditions – rules and traditions that may be at variance with the prescriptions of Holy Scripture. And then it becomes necessary to pull that culture together again.

This is no easy task. People get used to their (bad) habits. Traditions cannot be rooted out easily, even if these traditions are counterproductive and wrong. When certain harmful values and goals have taken root in an organization it is difficult to get rid of these and to replace them with better values and goals. It is, though, necessary because the culture of any church is supposed to be in accordance with the prescriptions of the Bible. Paul writes, for instance, in 1 Thess 2: 13 –

> "And for this cause we still give praise to God, that, when the word came to your ears through us, you took it, not as the word of man, but, as it truly is, the word of God, which has living power in you who have faith."

In other words, Paul had positive regard for the fact that this church had accepted the Gospel and lived according to it.

It often happens that churches endeavors to revive a moribund congregation by introducing various tricks – a noisy band, concerts during the Sunday service, liturgical innovations *etcetera*. It has to be remembered: the object of a Sunday service is not to entertain the congregation. The church is not part of the entertainment business. Unfortunately, many people expect the church to entertain them on a Sunday and they seek an interesting and exciting experience when they visit the church. It can be safely said that people with this attitude cannot be sincere in their faith.

When Christians gather in church on a Sunday, they have to realize that they are there to worship God, to be fed spiritually from the Word of God and to receive inspiration to go out and make a difference in the world in which they are living. A true reformation and an effective revival do not amount to emotional upheavals and pleasant experiences; it amounts to honest self-examination and a rededication to the cause of Jesus Christ. That can only be achieved where the Word of God is preached and disseminated effectively and truthfully.

The enthusiasm of the spiritual leader of the congregation for the calling of the church is the main motor to drive this reformation and revival. If he demonstrates his full commitment to the interests of the Kingdom of God then the congregation will inevitably follow.

26. PRODUCTIVE MEETINGS

Read: Acts 2: 15–25
What can we learn about productive meetings from this passage?

Chairing a Meeting

Managers and leaders must know how to chair a meeting. No church can function without regular meetings: meetings of the church council, various committees and teams who are tasked with certain activities. Even a Bible study group can be seen as a meeting and the leader of that group has to know how to lead that meeting.

There are various examples of meetings in the book of Acts where decisions had to be made collectively;

- In Acts 6: 1–7 we read that the apostles initially ran affairs in the Jerusalem congregation, but when they could not handle everything anymore a group of seven men were chosen by a meeting of the congregation to take over the management of the church, while the apostles concentrated on preaching, evangelizing and prayer.
- We encounter a body of elders in the Jerusalem church in Acts 11: 29-30 and Acts 15: 4-6. We are nowhere informed how this body was created and it may be assumed that they were the seven men chosen in Acts 6.
- The teachers and prophets of the church in Antioch had the habit of holding regular meetings where they prayed and fasted (Acts 13: 2).
- Paul convened a meeting of the elders of the church in Ephesus when he passed through the harbor of that city on his way to Jerusalem (Acts 20: 17).

- When Paul arrived in Jerusalem, he had a meeting with James, the leader of the congregation, as well as with the body of elders (Acts 21: 18).
- In Phil 1: 1 we read of the church council of the church in Philippi, consisting of the elders and deacons.

It is clear, therefore, that decisions in the church were taken collectively from the earliest times. Although there were people in leading positions in all the churches, the final authority lay with a body of believers, which may be seen as the church council of that church. There are also instances where the whole congregation was consulted (Acts 6: 5, 13: 3 and 15: 21).

The following rules may be helpful for the conduct of productive meetings:

- Every meeting needs at least a chairperson and a secretary. The task of the chairperson is to lead the meeting, keeping order and allocate turns for members to speak. The secretary's task is to keep the minutes and help the chair person to regulate things.
- Every meeting must have a clear agenda that has to be approved at the start of the meeting. Additional items can only be added at the start of the meeting with the approval of the meeting. It is not recommended that the item "General" appears on an agenda because that might open the door for unplanned and unwanted topics to be introduced and might lead to overhasty decisions.
- The compilation of the agenda is usually the task of the chair person and the secretary. This agenda is always provisional until it has been approved by the meeting. It is always possible that a meeting may decide not to discuss certain items on the provisional agenda, for whatever reason. The agenda usually contains reports by various individuals and committees

regarding their work, together with proposals and recommend-dations.

- The first item on any agenda must be to count those present. Do they constitute a quorum? Are there enough members present for the meeting to proceed? It is always a good idea to keep an attendance register that has to be signed by everybody present.

- The second item on any agenda must be to deal with requests for leave of absence.

- After the meeting has been duly constituted it has to be opened in an appropriate way – by reading a passage from Scripture and a prayer, or even a few prayers.

- The fourth item on the agenda of a regular meeting is the approval of the points on the agenda; does the meeting agree that the various items on the agenda need to be discussed? It is theoretically possible that a meeting may decide that a certain item is not part of their business.

- Next, the minutes of the previous regular meeting, as well as the minutes of any special meetings, have to be approved and signed by the chair and secretary on behalf of the meeting. It is always possible that the minutes of a previous meeting are incomplete or inaccurate and these flaws have to be corrected with the approval of the meeting.

- The sixth item on the agenda flows from the previous one. Are there any issues mentioned in the minutes that need more attention?

- A regular item on any agenda is financial matters – a report regarding the current financial state of the church. A budget for the coming year has to be approved at the first meeting before the completion of the financial year.

- It is always possible to call special or extraordinary meetings of the church council or another body in order to discuss urgent matters. Only these urgent matters are to be discussed at such a special meeting.

- The chairperson, secretary and all members must be prepared and study the agenda thoroughly beforehand. It may help to do some extra research about certain items on the agenda so as to serve the meeting with accurate information.

- Use visual aids to illustrate and explain certain difficult points (for example a PowerPoint presentation, graphs etcetera).

- Know the procedures to be followed. It is important that every proposal or recommendation be seconded by another member of the meeting – otherwise it cannot be discussed and voted upon. If it is necessary to conduct a vote on any matter the votes for and against the proposal have to be counted. If the proposal does not get a majority of the votes, it cannot be adopted.

- Know how to deal with difficult (talkative, demanding and aggressive) members of the meeting; the most effective method is to allow other members of the meeting to silence them.

- Give everybody a chance to take part in a discussion, but prevent a situation where two or more people talk simultaneously. It may be a good thing to have a rule that every member of a larger meeting has one opportunity to speak when a certain item on the agenda is to be discussed. In smaller and informal committee meetings it may be possible for members to speak their minds more often.

- Know how to save time.

- It is better to lead a meeting to consensus rather than making people vote.

- Give a summary of the most important ideas at the end of a discussion, bringing any debate to a close by drawing certain conclusions and giving the members an idea of the alternatives between which they have to choose.

- The minutes of a meeting are not to be confused with a report about a meeting. The minutes only contain the names of those present, the names of those who asked for leave of absence, proposals and decisions of the meeting. Reports by individuals or committees regarding their activities can be annexed to the minutes for future reference if they were not included in the agenda. The speeches of members are not to be summarized. The minutes have to be approved at the next meeting as an accurate rendering of the actions of the previous meeting.

27. MANAGING COMMITTEES AND TEAMS

Read: Acts 13: 1–4; Acts 14: 27; Acts 15: 2 & 30; 2 Cor 8: 16–24
What can we learn about committees and deputies of churches from these passages?

Organizing Committees and Teams

Any organization consists of subgroups – committees, task groups or teams. It is an essential element of administering and managing the church to get these subsystems to work effectively. Management often boils down to grouping and arranging groups of people to accomplish certain goals.

Some groups may be formed to perform a specific task, such as planning a building project, after which this team or committee may be disbanded. Other groups may be of a more permanent nature, depending on the tasks delegated to them.

Delegation of Tasks

It is impossible for a church council or a pastor of priest to micro-manage all affairs in the church. It is, therefore, necessary to deputize certain persons to perform certain tasks. These tasks may be delegated to individuals or committees or teams.

Many church councils have committees that deal with the following aspects of the life of the church:

- Sunday worship and the music ministry.
- Youth affairs.
- Financial matters.
- The maintenance of immovable property.

- Evangelism and missions.
- Charitable work (usually, the deacons deal with this aspect)
- The maintenance of discipline in the church (this is one of the tasks of the elders).
- The work of women in the church.
- There may also be an executive committee to deal with urgent matters that cannot wait until the next scheduled meeting of the church council.
- It may also be necessary to appoint an *ad hoc* committee to investigate a certain matter or to deal with an unexpected unique emergency.

Although these persons and groups receive mandates to perform certain functions it must always be remembered that the final responsibility lies with the church council as the governing body of the congregation. Therefore, all the deputized individuals and committees have to report back to the church council regularly regarding their activities. In this regard, we have the example of Paul and Barnabas, two of the teachers of the church in Antioch, who were chosen to undertake a missionary outreach (Acts 13: 1-4). When they had completed their travels, they reported back to those who had sent them out (Acts 14: 27).

It is a sound management principle that no governing body may relinquish its authority and give power of attorney to certain individuals or committees to take over their responsibilities. That may also not happen in the church and it amounts to an abdication of its responsibilities.

The Management of Teams and Committees
The work in a church is, to a very large extent, dependent upon the efforts of volunteers, the lay members of the church. The church

council and all its committees or deputies are all comprised of voluntary workers. These people are usually assembled into committees and teams according to their own fields of interest and their availability. There is, therefore, little control over the composition of committees, although their membership has eventually to be approved by the church council. In synods, conferences, councils, presbyteries, circuits and other meetings of the church in a wider context, the composition of committees is usually a more formal affair and people are voted into certain positions on account of their expertise and experience.

Since team members have to work in close proximity, have to co-ordinate their efforts and are dependent on each other it is necessary that they be trained to work together. Their personalities, level of motivation, value systems and disciplinary records should receive consideration.

High-performing teams usually exhibit an overall team purpose, mutual accountability, collective work, shared leadership roles, high cohesiveness and group loyalty, collaboration in choosing procedures, collective task assignment and collective assessment of their own successes and failures.

The cohesiveness of a team can be improved by team building exercises – when necessary – where the necessary skills are taught and where members learn to trust each other. During team building exercises teams ought to get greater clarity on the following questions:

- Who are we?
- What are our tasks?
- Which skills and aptitudes are available?
- How are we to perform our work?
- How do we know when we perform as expected?

- Are there better methods for performing our tasks?
- How can we improve?
- How can we enjoy our team more?

The success of a team or committee is dependent upon the following:

- An enthusiastic and inspired leader;
- A supportive environment;
- Clear objectives and goals;
- A clear division of tasks and roles; and
- Enough opportunity for communication and interaction.

A successful team or committee has the following attributes:

- A clear vision of the future which inspires everybody;
- A clear goal which is pursued by all members of the team;
- Clarity on who are members of the team and who are not;
- Strong leadership by an inspired and competent leader;
- Enjoyment by members of their membership of the team and willing co-operation;
- Mutual trust;
- Collective ownership and responsibility for the outputs of the team;
- Consensus on values, roles, plans of action and working methods;
- Good communication within the team and with the environment;
- The necessary skills and knowledge to successfully perform the tasks assigned to the team;
- Flexibility and the willingness to learn new skills and adopt new procedures;

- A willingness to improve performance; and
- Internal management of all matters pertaining to the team.

It is necessary that teams and committees operate on the basis of consensus. Consensus may be reached in one or more of the following ways:

- Everybody agrees;
- Everybody agrees to differ;
- Only those team members or subgroups who are influenced by the outcome of a decision participate in the decision-making process;
- When votes are taken those in the minority agree to abide by the decision of the majority; or
- Everybody agrees that those with dissenting votes should come with practical alternative plans or courses of action.

28. PERFORMANCE APPRAISALS

Read: Matt 7: 24–27; 1 Cor 3: 9–15
How important is the quality of your work in the church?

Any program to improve the performance of church workers (and employees) will be useless unless a system for the measurement of performance is also adopted. If the quality of work is to be improved, it is necessary that one knows what the current levels of performance are. Performance must also be measured on future occasions in order to determine whether any improvement has occurred.

The measurement of the performance of workers and teams is not always so straightforward since we are dealing with human beings, each with his own individuality and limitations.

What is Performance Appraisal?
Performance *appraisal* may be defined as follows:

> Performance appraisal is a formal discussion between a supervisor or a panel of observers and a worker or a team of workers for the purpose of discovering how the worker or team is performing on the job and how this performance can be made more effective and efficient so that the supervisor, the worker or the team and the organization all will benefit.

The Goals of Performance Appraisal
The general goal of a system of performance appraisal is to determine as accurately as possible the current level of the effectiveness and efficiency or workers or teams with the aim of

improving their performance. This goal may be subdivided into the following:

- It must be determined whether an employee's remuneration is in accordance with his or her performance;
- It must be determined whether a worker or team needs more training and development in order to perform more productively and to eliminate any mistakes made;
- The implementation of a performance appraisal system helps the leadership and the workforce to get greater clarity on performance standards;
- Through a system of performance appraisal church management can evaluate the effectiveness of training programs; and
- The need of workers to know where they stand in the organization is satisfied through the process of appraisal.

It is to be recommended that supervisors keep a record of all sessions with those they supervise and the outcome of these sessions. In this manner, a paper trail of all the complaints, mistakes, achievements, instructions, counselling and praise in respect of a certain worker is created and that helps church management to compile an assessment report at the right time.

A system of performance appraisal can only work if all the stakeholders have agreed on a set of performance standards. It is only possible to evaluate the work of an individual or team when there is clarity about the standard of work expected of them.

Methods of Performance Appraisal

A fairly large number of performance appraisal systems have been devised over the years. There are only two systems that really work:

- *Direct methods: the measurement of outputs:*

This is a simple procedure in cases where an employee's output can be measured directly and accurately. It is a relatively straightforward procedure to count the number of visits the pastor or elder made to parishioners during the period in question and how often other activities were undertaken.

- *Behavioral observation scales:*

This is the method of choice where it is not possible to measure outputs directly. According to this system a rater or a panel of raters judge the quality and quantity of work, as well as the worker's ability to perform the job, on a rating scale. This scale must be based on the worker's job description and on a job specification.

The following types of items must appear on the scale:

- The most important and most crucial tasks to be performed by the worker;
- The type of behaviors that must be exhibited while performing the job (*i e* the methods and procedures to be followed);
- The most important abilities and skills required for the job in question; and
- A list of achievements and mistakes that the person made during the preceding period and steps taken to remedy these mistakes.

The rater(s) must then judge how well the worker performed the tasks mentioned and to what extent he or she has the required behaviors, abilities and skills.

Experience has also shown that employers are mostly only interested in the following: are the work, behavior and abilities of the worker *unacceptable, acceptable* or *excellent*? A three-point scale with these three anchors is easily administered and gives results that are more accurate, since no comparison with the hypothetical and non-existent "average worker" is made.

Self-Appraisal

It is necessary to say something regarding self-appraisal.

In many cases, it is not possible for a supervisor to appraise the work of an employee because this work is not performed in an observable or visible manner. Most workers usually know fairly accurately how well or how poorly they perform. If there is a trusting relationship between the rating panel and the employee it is possible that the employee will give an honest evaluation of his or her own work. Of course, there is always the temptation to present one's own work in a more positive light, but a supervisor who knows his or her subordinates will be aware of this tendency.

The Procedure to be Followed During Appraisals

Appraisals usually follow the following procedure:

- The church council or management decides to evaluate the performance of the work force and appoints somebody to conduct or lead the exercise;
- If the appraisal is to be performed by a panel, the members of the panel are selected. Three or four members of the church council may be tasked with this enterprise.
- This leader or the panel decides on a method and a strategy for conducting the appraisal;
- The chosen method is applied and its implementation is monitored in order to ascertain whether this method lives up to expectations;
- Information that is gained is evaluated and interpreted;
- A decision is taken regarding the method of dissemination of the information; and
- All interested parties – management and employees – are informed regarding the results of their appraisal.

The confidential feedback interview should be conducted as soon as possible after the appraisal. The worker or employee must be given an ample opportunity to state his or her case and to give reasons why he or she does not agree with a certain finding in the evaluation or to give reasons for an unsatisfactory performance.

The interview should focus on finding solutions for the problems identified and the worker or employee must have an opportunity to participate in the finding of possible solutions. It is desirable that the worker declare his or her commitment to the proposed solution. Areas in which the worker or employee needs development or further training should be dealt with in the same manner.

It is important, once again, to remember that the church is a voluntary organization. Elders, deacons and other workers do their work in their spare time and, therefore, no undue pressure can be placed on them to perform better or work longer hours. The appraisal of their performance should have the overriding goal of motivating them to perform better and to work smarter. In the case of employees, such as the pastor/minister/priest or administrative staff, they may be rated according to the requirements set in their contracts of employment.

That the church cannot forego a system of performance appraisal is clear from Jesus' parable of the talents (Matt 25: 14-30). The owner of three slaves went on a journey and gave each slave a certain amount of talents to work with. At his return, he required each of them to report back to him regarding their efforts and he either praised the industrious slaves and rebuked the lazy slave. That is nothing but a system of work evaluation propagated by Jesus.

29. THE MANAGEMENT OF HUMAN RELATIONS IN THE CHURCH

No leader in the church can get along without good human relationships. The leader with bad human relationships will repel and even insult people and he won't be in the position to provide effective leadership and management.

Read: 1 Cor 13
Answer the following questions:
- *Does life have any meaning without love? (vs 1–3)*
- *Describe the characteristics of love (vs 4–7)*
- *Why is love eternal? (vs 8–13)*
- *How can we obtain love?*

Read: Rom 12: 9–20
What can we learn about good human relationships from this passage?

Any person can apply the following principles and techniques in a wide variety of situations in order to improve his interpersonal relationships. This is especially necessary for people in leading positions in the church:

- Use the names of other people frequently. Certain leaders do so almost never.
- Remember that appreciation and recognition bring out the best in people; on the other hand, unfair criticism tends to bring out the worst.

- Be an easy-going person in the company of others: stay cheerful and pleasant at all times – even if you do not feel cheerful.
- If you fall for the temptation to argue with somebody, remember that no two people perceive the world in the same manner. Grant them the right to be different.
- Avoid topics with a depressive or negative content, or topics which others may find offensive or threatening. There are people who complain about everything. Rather make it a habit of talking about positive things.
- Give people the benefit of the doubt if they hurt your feelings. It seldom happens that people deliberately intend to insult or hurt. They are often only busy boosting their own self-image or solving their own problems and you just happen to be in the way.
- Do not tire other people with your problems. People tend to avoid those who are always complaining. Remember, everybody has problems, even if you do not know about them.
- Be sensitive to the moods of others. Choose your remarks and actions to fit those people's feelings.
- Empower people and make them feel more capable by showing them that you have full confidence in their abilities and skills.
- Avoid controversial topics in the company of strangers, such as politics.
- Do not humiliate people by criticizing them in front of others.
- Respect the good reputation of others and show them that you expect them to maintain their good standing. Do not attribute unworthy motives to others. Nobody is perfect, but nobody likes it when their mistakes are continuously being pointed out.
- Take some trouble to help others.
- Greet people in a friendly and cheerful manner and show that you are glad to see them.
- Practice to be a good listener.

- Go out of your way to make others feel important. A simple method is to enquire about their thoughts on certain issues and to ask their opinions generally.
- Preserve your sense of humor and be prepared to laugh at yourself. Be careful of being frivolous where it is inappropriate.
- Keep confidential information to yourself; you would certainly not like it if other people gossiped about you and shared your secrets.
- Respect other people's eccentricities; we all have some.
- When people irritate you, it is better not to show it.
- Be dependable and do not make any promises you cannot keep.
- Make sure to always say "thank you" and to show your gratitude when somebody does something for you.
- Inform people about compliments and positive comments that other people have made about them.
- Be generous with your compliments regarding the achievements of others.
- Follow the example of Jesus who always had time for sick people, lepers, blind people, children, fallen women, criminals and lonely people.

From the foregoing the following become clear:

- Good human relationships flourish in an atmosphere of neighborly love and mutual trust;
- Good human relationships are built upon respect for the human dignity of others;
- If the human relationships in a church are not up to scratch the motivation of members will disappear and the church may stagnate; and

- Good human relationships also entail civility, politeness, consideration of the needs and problems of others and good manners.

30. THE MANAGEMENT OF CONFLICT IN THE CHURCH

The situation may arise in which a leader in the church is required to solve conflict and to deal with hostility between people. It may also be that the leader finds himself in an explosive situation with difficult people, where conflict may erupt. How must one go about solving the conflict or preventing the conflict from escalating?

Read: Matt 5: 43–48
Now answer the following questions:
- *Why is it, according to Jesus, necessary that we love our enemies?*
- *What example does our heavenly Father give us?*
- *Who are our enemies?*
- *Is it easy to love our enemies?*
- *Is it required of us to like our enemies?*
- *What must we do to love our enemies?*
- *What happens when we love our enemies?*

Ineffective Ways of Dealing with Conflict
The following ways of acting in a conflict situation are unproductive and ineffective:

- *Placate:* This approach entails keeping the peace at all costs, seeking to placate the adversaries and wanting them to surrender in the face of demands. Nobody respects a person who throws in the towel, and no problems are solved in this manner. The person who always placates others and surrenders easily also loses his or her self-respect. All it signals is a condoning of the dishonest methods of the adversaries.

- *Competition:* The feuding parties try to win at all costs and protect their interests, even if it means annihilating the other party. Of course, nobody succeeds in destroying the other side and the animosity between them just continues.

- *Ignore:* Differences and clashes are swept under the rug as if they never existed. What this means is that the differences keep simmering under the surface and no solutions are ever reached.

- *Compromise:* An effort is made to satisfy all the parties and create a so-called win-win situation. Everyone is expected to relinquish certain demands and expectations – but this only leads to dissatisfaction and resentment.

- *Defend and counter-attack:* If we are attacked or criticized, we tend to fight back and defend ourselves. This only escalates the conflict.

- *Accusations:* Any situation with conflict is the result of a complex series of causes. To hold only one party responsible for all the problems is unfair and leads to injustice.

All these methods are incompatible with the lesson Jesus wanted to teach his followers in Matt 5: 43–48.

There are, though, much better ways of dealing with conflict and the following strategies ought to be helpful:

Identify the Needs of the Parties

If the leader succeeds in getting the opposing parties to sit around a table to find a solution to their differences, then a set of rules for the conversation ought to be agreed upon by the parties. Examples of these rules are as follows:

- Afford everybody a reasonable chance to say what he or she wants to say;
- Do not interrupt a speaker;
- The chair keeps order and allots speaking turns;
- Avoid insults and personal attacks; and
- If the parties consist of more than one person then every party has to have a spokesperson who speaks on behalf of the group.

It is important to know in a conflict situation what the needs and desires of the warring parties are – these may often differ from the explicit demands they have placed on their adversaries. The following have to be determined:

- Is it possible that all they need is to be heard with understanding?
- Do they merely have a need for recognition or encouragement?
- Do they need opportunities to realize their plans and ideals?
- What are their interests and rights in the situation?
- Do they have moral principles, plans and ideals that cannot be realized?
- Which emotions have been stirred up by the situation?

To get to the root of the problem, listen empathetically and constructively to uncover the parties' frustrations, expectations, hopes, disappointments, and needs. Reflect remarks with an emotional content back to the speakers with the goal of helping them to talk more about their feelings and needs. If they get the feeling that the mediator understands how they feel they will be much more willing to listen to his suggestions and proposals later on.

This does not mean that the mediator must necessarily agree with everything he hears. If he listens with empathy, however, the parties receive the message that their feelings are being understood, that the mediator acknowledges their right to have certain feelings and that they are allowed to have rights, interests and needs. In this manner, bridges are built between the mediator and the parties.

It is necessary for the mediator to stay impartial at all times. He should not in any way create the impression that he favors one party over the other. This means that he must avoid all forms of criticism or advice; at most, he may ask questions and make suggestions when he thinks that one party is acting unethically. He may, however, impart factual information, including what the law provides regarding a certain issue.

Identify the Reasons for the Conflict

After the needs, interests, wishes and rights of each antagonistic party has been identified, it becomes easier to see why these needs, interests, wishes and rights are in opposition. The mediator has, subsequently, to pay attention to the following questions:

- Do the parties want the same thing?
- Do any of the parties wish for something that may have an adverse impact on the interests and needs of the other party?
- Will the demands and wishes of one party harm the other party?

Where there is a direct clash of interests, rights and needs, destructive conflict may easily erupt. If one party is stronger than the other, then that party may enforce its interests, rights and needs at the expense of the other party. The aggrieved party may try to take revenge by means of sabotage, the withholding of information, the twisting of information, the spread of malicious rumors and insubordination.

This state of affairs will never facilitate good human relationships or the smooth functioning of any organization.

Identify the Ultimate Outcome

After the problem(s) have been identified, it is important to hear from the parties what type of outcome they would like to have. What result do they wish from the mediation process?

If everybody agrees that it is desirable that peace and cordial relationships be restored then there is something on which everybody agrees and that makes cooperation towards that goal so much easier.

In a church setting, it will also be important to hear from all parties that they wish the church to flourish. That may be a unifying aspect.

Ask for Possible Solutions

Any mediator trying to defuse a conflict situation will find that it is profitable to invite the parties to suggest solutions for the clash of interests, rights and needs. This conveys the message that the opinion or point of view of each party is important. Once the needs, wishes, demands, rights and interests of everybody have been identified, the referee, facilitator or mediator should ask the parties to suggest possible solutions for the resolution of the conflict – instead of trying to determine who is right and who is wrong as a judge would do.

This means that the possible solutions receive more attention than the nature of the problem. If the problem or point being disputed receives too much attention, it may cause the parties' perceptions of the problem to escalate, and they may fight harder to justify their point of view. It may help to focus more on the possible solutions and to focus attention on the areas where the parties may rather cooperate in order to reach a solution.

It is important to remember that parties in a conflict tend to expect their adversaries to make all the concessions as part of the proposed solution. The mediator ought to ask all the participants for suggestions how they are willing to change their demands, methods and expectations in order to defuse the situation. Placing pressure on the adversaries will only create counter-pressure. It is better if each party is willing to ask itself: what can we do to improve the situation?

Discuss the Proposed Solutions

After the parties have tabled possible solutions, these proposals have to be discussed. It must be determined how each proposal will affect all the parties and whether it can be executed in practice.

The facilitator should keep any criticism of proposals impersonal and factual. If criticism takes the form of personal attacks, nothing is gained and the fight will simply continue, while at least one of the parties will lose trust in the facilitator's impartiality. If the issues are discussed and weighed up in a rational manner, then progress can be made.

Both parties have to be led to the insight that their adversaries have legitimate rights, interests, needs, demands, and wishes. The next step is to explore common ground:

- On which issues do the parties have agreement?
- Which goals, values, and principles do they share?

Use the common ground to progressively reach consensus about more issues. It may be the case that both parties are willing to make concessions to broaden the common ground and to lessen the number of disputed points – and even possibly eliminate them in the end.

It is always a good thing to identify common goals and values of the parties. If they share a common vision and common principles and feel loyal towards the church to which they belong, they may be encouraged to see each other as allies instead of opponents or adversaries. The mediator should create an atmosphere where the parties realize that they are part of a greater "we", instead of seeing themselves as "us" versus "them".

Furthermore, this cooperative style of dealing with conflict uses one or more of the following techniques:

- *Let off steam:* give the warring parties the opportunity to state their cases comprehensively and to vent their frustrations and anger to the full extent. If they get the impression that their concerns are being heard it may lead to greater calm and rationality.
- *Negotiation:* The contesting factions are encouraged to listen to each other and to understand the other side's point of view. This may lead to the abandonment of spurious and excessive claims.
- *Confrontation:* The competing parties jointly launch an honest investigation into the reasons for the conflict and to find common ground. This must lead to –
    o Plans for the solution of clashes of interests;
    o A solution that is acceptable to both sides; and
    o A clear commitment of the parties to cooperate in future.

Prevent Conflict

It is always preferable to prevent destructive conflict as far as possible.

There are, naturally, cases where constructive conflict may occur and this must be managed with care to prevent it from deteriorating into destructive conflict. Many organizations mount planning sessions or think-tanks to devise strategies for the future. The participants are encouraged to mention all their thoughts, worries, fears, complaints, needs, rights (as they see them), ideals and expectations in a safe atmosphere and from there to move in the direction of innovative solutions and plans. Although large differences of opinion often occur, the chair or facilitator must see to it that the participants do not make personal comments about each other and that they deal with their differing opinions in a reasonable way. It may be expected of the speakers to provide reasons for their opinions in order to prevent time being wasted with unmotivated and wild statements, and to prevent the feelings of other participants being hurt.

Destructive conflict must, however, be prevented as far as possible. This may be achieved by fostering a trusting relationship between individuals and groups within the church. This may occur where people are recognized and respected as individuals – each with his own personality, needs, and rights. Stable and sound relationships are in everybody's interest, and these may be nurtured where the rights, interests, ideals, expectations, wishes, fears and worries of each person or party is recognized and respected. Provision must be made for the social needs of the parties by providing for their needs for recognition, stimulation, and security.

The pastoral mediator must apply the human relationship laws (see the previous chapter) in order to promote the peaceful co-existence of groups and persons who may become embroiled in disputes. It can be a very satisfying and enriching experience to help defuse conflict.

Remember what Jesus said: "Blessed are the peacemakers: for they shall be called the children of God" (Matt 5: 9).

31. THE USE OF TECHNOLOGY

The technology available to Jesus and the apostles was minimal. They had to travel on foot, on the back of donkey or by means of a sailing ship. Paul and the other apostles had to write their letters by hand or dictate them to a secretary. These letters were to be delivered to their destinations by a courier who happened to travel in that direction. For instance: while Paul was in Corinth, he wrote his letter to the church in Rome. This letter was taken thither by a deaconess, a woman named Phoebe (Rom 16: 1 & 2).

In our time, the church has wonderful opportunities to serve the kingdom of God by embracing available technology and institutions. There is electrical lighting, telephones, mobile phones, fax machines, computers with sophisticated software (amongst others, for financial management), electronic mail and the internet, motorized transport, watches, public address systems, modern building techniques to be used when erecting new church buildings, banks to deposit money, *etcetera*. There is absolutely nothing wrong with the church taking advantage of these marvels of technology. They can be time-saving, improve effectiveness and efficiency and help the church to disseminate its message so much more easily.

Many churches made very good use of social media during 2020–2021 when the Corona Virus pandemic, also known as Covid-19, caused the world to come to a standstill. Most countries restricted the movement of their citizens and prohibited all meetings, including religious gatherings. Churches could stay in touch with their members through social media and sermons could be streamed through programs such as Zoom. Without this access to modern technology, may congregations would have been totally paralyzed.

32. THE SPIRITUAL AND PSYCHOLOGICAL HEALTH OF CHURCH LEADERS

Read: 1 Sam 19: 9–10 & 31: 4–6; I Kgs 19: 3–5
What can you tell about the psychological/emotional and spiritual health of King Saul and Elijah?

It is often asked: "How does a normal and happy person look? What are the qualities of a person who has managed to develop his human dignity fully?" It is necessary for the church leader to be aware of the answers to these questions because it is one of his tasks to lead people to spiritual and psychological health. It is also necessary for the leader to ask himself: "How is my own spiritual and psychological health?"

Psychological Wrecks

An easy answer to the questions above is: somebody who functions well on a spiritual and psychological level is somebody who does not suffer from some or other psychological disorder. He is, therefore, not a psychological wreck.

But that does not tell us very much. Medical doctors often struggle with the question: When is somebody physically healthy? Is it only when there is an absence of pain, fever or other medical complaints, or is it more than that?

Physical health is more than only the absence of an ailment. It might be that somebody does not have fever, does not feel any pain and does not suffer from some or other physical deformity, but it might also be that he does not have much energy, sleeps badly or complains of shortness of breath. In that case, one may say that that person's health is not what it should be. To be really healthy one has to have enough energy and strength, one has to have a functioning immune system and one must be able to enjoy life.

And in the same vein, psychological health is much more than just the absence of psychological problems and complaints.

Defining Qualities

The following nine qualities or characteristics may be regarded as defining spiritual and psychological health:

1. Control over emotions
2. Control over drives and impulses
3. Self-knowledge
4. Realistic optimism
5. Self confidence
6. Empathy
7. Compassion
8. Humor
9. A fixed philosophy of life

Each one of these characteristics has to be explained:

Control over Emotions

The first characteristic is *control over emotions*. To have that you have to know your own emotional state. You must recognize whether you are angry, glad, disappointed, irritated, stressed or bored. And then you also have to be able to judge whether these emotions are fitting in the situation in which you are. People very often have very inappropriate emotions in certain situations.

If your friend arrives late for an appointment, it might be inappropriate to be furious; it would, perhaps, be more appropriate to be merely irritated or disappointed. Should you be furious and you tell him in no uncertain terms what a bad specimen of the human species he is, your friendship will definitely be ruined. If you inform him in a calm way that you are disappointed and inconvenienced by him coming late then you also give him the opportunity to explain why he could not make it earlier and even apologize for his failure to be on time. Should you act in this manner then you will have demonstrated control over your emotions without acting in a childish or egotistical manner.

In other words: the person who is functioning well is somebody who can control he feelings and knows how to give vent to these feelings in certain situations. A human being is, after all, a free being who can choose how to act and react.

Jesus certainly had this characteristic. We read very little in the Bible regarding his emotions. We know that he wept when He heard about the death of his friend Lazarus. He became justifiably angry when money lenders and retailers abused the temple complex in Jerusalem to make dishonest profits. We also read that He had time for people who did not count for much in those times – women, tax collectors, cripples, blind people and children. Jesus must have had excellent control over his emotions.

Control over drives and impulses

The second quality is *control over drives and impulses*. To state it somewhat differently: the ability to withstand temptations and practice self-control and restraint. We all have certain drives. We need nutrition, water, warmth, rest and oxygen to live. We need relaxation, sleep, company and excitement. But it is not always possible to satisfy these needs immediately – except for the need to breathe and get oxygen. That is something that has to be satisfied constantly. But the satisfaction of the other needs can usually wait, if needs be.

And the mature, balanced person knows how to satisfy these needs in an appropriate way. You do not fall asleep in company – you wait until it becomes bed time and you can reach your own bed. You will not seek relaxation in front of the television while you have visitors – you switch the television off in order to pay attention to your guests.

Therefore – the mature and balanced individual is somebody who takes control over his life and drives and is able to postpone the satisfaction of his needs. This amounts to emotional intelligence.

Self-Knowledge

The third trait is *self-knowledge*. The person with a mature, balanced and well-rounded personality knows and understands himself. He knows what his strong and weak points are. He knows what he can do and cannot do. He is informed about his own abilities and restraints and he will, therefore, not make a fool of himself by trying to do impossible things. He also knows, though, whether he has a realistic chance to tackle a certain challenge and make a success of it.

He acknowledges his guilt if something goes wrong and he does not try to hide behind feeble excuses. Somebody with self-knowledge is, therefore, aware of the sources of his problems and failures – also when he contributed to these problems and failures. He will, therefore, not blame other people for his problems and failures.

Jesus must have had this quality. We often read in the Gospels that He performed miracles. He healed sick people. He restored the sight of blind people. He resurrected dead people. He walked on water. He commanded storms to quieten down. He fed a multitude of people. But there also were opportunities where He declined to perform miracles. That was when the people with whom

He was dealing at that moment did not trust Him or when people asked Him only for the sake of sensation to perform signs and miracles. Jesus, therefore, knew when He could perform a miracle and when He could not do it. He knew Himself well.

Realistic Optimism

The fourth characteristic is *realistic optimism*. The person who functions well psychologically is also an optimistic person. Somebody who is chronically pessimistic and always expects bad things from the future most probably has one or other psychological problem, such as depression, an anxiety disorder or a personality disorder. The mature and balanced human being always sees the bright side of life. For him the proverbial glass is always half full – not half empty. He is also able to look at life realistically. He makes certain of his facts and does not jump to overhasty conclusions in order to prevent him from making a fool of himself.

Jesus was also such an optimistic and realistic person. He must have had a very good insight into human nature and He could easily see when people acted with hidden agendas. Although He made a number of predictions about the future regarding calamities and tribulations in his prophetic sermon and warned the faithful that they must expect persecution and suffering, He was generally an optimist. He had great trust in his Father in heaven and, therefore, He continuously did good to people in need.

Self-Confidence

There also is *self-confidence*. This is to a certain extent related to self-knowledge. The person with self-confidence knows that he can weather any number of storms in his life, that he will be able to solve problems in his life and that he will be able to handle most situations. This type of person is self-sufficient and does not need to rely constantly on other people to help him. This is somebody who can act independently and stand on his own feet.

There are people with a so-called dependent personality disorder. They constantly seek the approval and assistance of others. They do not see their way clear to do anything on their own and others must push them to achieve something. The adult and balanced person does not need this. He is able to tackle challenges, to take initiative and to remain standing when the storms of life threaten to blow him over.

Throughout the Gospels it becomes clear that Jesus acted with self-confidence and without fear. He did not shy away from anybody, although there were enough people who tried to obstruct Him. One can hardly think of a better example of self-confidence. Please note that self-confidence must not be confused with haughtiness, arrogance or aggression. Although Jesus demonstrated much self-confidence, He never became haughty or arrogant. He always acted with love and thoughtfulness.

Empathy

One cannot forget *empathy*. That means that you are able to imagine yourself in the situation and feelings of somebody else. You are able to interpret the feelings of others accurately. You can discern whether they are frustrated, angry, sad, disappointed, depressive or afraid. And then you can understand how that person feels. You know how it must feel to be standing in that person's shoes. Paul writes in Rom 12:15 – "Take part in the joy of those who are glad, and in the grief of those who are sorrowing."

One can be sure that Jesus had this characteristic of empathy. He understood the feelings of others. He knew when people were feeling lonely, sad, rejected or guilty – and then He had fitting words for that person. That is why the crowds followed Him and wanted to hear every word from his lips. They must have felt that He was somebody who understood them in their poverty and suffering, who had a message for them in their situation of oppression, despair and neediness.

Compassion

The seventh quality is the quality of *compassion*. This is something akin to empathy because it is the action that follows empathy. Somebody who really has empathy with others will inevitably also have compassion and that means that he also something about that person's situation.

If you have compassion, you are willing to make your time and energy available to others – people who have some or urgent need or who cannot help themselves. The person with compassion is able to reach out to others, take their hands and help to find solutions for their problems and pains.

This was without doubt one of Jesus' characteristics. We read in the Gospels of three aspects of his life. The Gospels devote much space to his trial and death on the cross. His death and his resurrection form the climax of each of the four Gospels. In the second place, the Gospels devoted much attention to his sermons and stories.

And in the third place we are informed of how He did good to others – often only by offering his attention and friendship to vulnerable people such as women, children, the sick, cripples and tax collectors. He had time for those were oppressed and neglected by others or were regarded as outcasts. On occasion, He even performed miracles to help people in their need. He healed the sick, fed the hungry, restored sight to the blind and brought to life the dead. One cannot think of a better example of somebody who had compassion than Jesus.

Humor

The balanced and happy person also has a sense of *humor*. This is the ability to laugh at yourself and at life in general. It is healthy to laugh because it helps you to forget your stresses and worries. If you can laugh at yourself and your troubles these problems all of a sudden do not look so serious and unmanageable anymore.

Few people realize it, but Jesus had a wonderful sense of humor and He often told jokes. Unfortunately, we do not always recognize his jokes for what they are.

It may be good to repeat two of his jokes. He told the story of this man who wanted to remove the splinter from the eye of his brother while failing to realize that he had a big log in his own eye (Matt 7: 3-5). This was, of course, greatly exaggerated. Please imagine a man with a huge log lodged in his eye! And He also said that it is easier for a camel to climb through the eye of a needle than it is for a rich man to get into heaven. Try and imagine how big a camel is and how small the eye of a needle is and you will realize that Jesus also utilized an absurd example in this instance (Matt 19:24). We can be sure that his audience must have laughed out aloud.

Fixed Philosophy of Life

A *fixed philosophy of life* is the last quality of somebody with good psychological functioning. Each of us has the need to discover meaning in life. We want to know: Where do I fit in? What is the goal of my life? What does God expect from me? How must I understand life? How must I understand all the calamities and accidents that torture me? How must I understand and overcome setbacks and disappointments?

The need to discover meaning in life is surely the deepest need in any person's existence. If something makes sense it seems to be easier to handle. We as Christians believe that we can find answers to all these questions in the Word of God.

Each of us also has the need to know what is right and wrong, as well as what is good and bad. The Lord gave each of us a conscience and the adult and balanced person does not like to violate his conscience by being guilty of unacceptable, ugly or bad behavior. We also believe that we find clear instructions for our behavior in the Bible – for instance, in the Ten Commandments and in Jesus' Sermon on the Mount. But each of us has received a conscience, which reminds us of what is good and bad or right and wrong. The Lord has, after all, written his law in the hearts and minds of people (Rom 2: 14 – 16).

In other words, the adult, normal and balanced individual has discovered meaning in life and he has an explanation of how things work in creation. That person also knows which behaviors are acceptable or unacceptable and he lives according to the dictates of his conscience. He, therefore, has a clear philosophy of life.

And one can also see these attributes in the life of Jesus. It has already been mentioned that large parts of the Gospels are devoted to his sermons and stories – and also his jokes! His stories dealt with everyday events, of situations that his audience would immediately have recognized as part of their world. But He did not tell these stories only to entertain people. Every story, parable and joke had a clear spiritual message and made something clear something about God and his kingdom.

On other occasions Jesus delivered more abstract sermons and explained certain important life principles – including in his Sermon on the Mount and his prophetic sermon. It is, therefore, clear that Jesus had a set of clear convictions. We must remember that He was a Jew and that He enjoyed a Jewish upbringing and education. He knew the Old Testament very well and He conveyed its message in a fresh and original way to his audience. Jesus spoke a lot about the kingdom of God. That means that we have to acknowledge God as the king or supreme authority in our lives.

We cannot go wrong if we adopt the philosophy of life that Jesus taught.

Freedom and Responsibility

It is possible to summarize these nine qualities of a person with good psychological health with two words: freedom and responsibility.

The free person who has control over his life and who knows where he is headed in life is also a person with a sense of responsibility. Although every one of us experiences the influences of a variety of factors in his life and he in confronted by situations over which he has little or no control, he stays a being with freedom of choice. He can make decisions and make choices – although his needs, emotions and relationships, of course, also have an influence on these choices and decisions. His principles will also have an influence and that sets he apart as a responsible being who is open to the spiritual dimensions in life.

33. EFFECTIVE TIME MANAGEMENT

Read: Gen 1: 1; Ps 90: 12–17; John 1: 1; Rev 22: 20.
Where does time come from? How must our attitude towards time be?

It is possible that certain workers in the church may be very busy and work long hours but do not necessarily fill those hours with the correct tasks. If those workers constantly perform irrelevant work that has little relationship with the primary goals of their jobs or tasks, they simply are not effective.

To be effective, a worker does not necessarily have to work longer hours; that worker, though, has to utilize the available time optimally. Some workers, however, have no control over their work pace:

- For instance, a factory worker who is supposed to receive an unfinished product from somebody else, to perform certain tasks on it and then to pass that product on to another worker, has to adjust to the pace of the chain of workers.
- The work pace of a team is, likewise, dependent on the inputs of all the members.

Many employees, on the other hand, have more discretion about the use of their time. One of the biggest sources of stress is time. When people feel that they have no control over the way they spend their time and when they have to meet looming deadlines, they get stressed. On the other hand, if one knows how to manage his time and utilizes his hours and minutes productively and effectively, he may keep his stress at bay. Good time management takes the following principles into consideration:

- Nobody can manage his or her time effectively without a proper diary – whether electronic or on paper. All the tasks that have to be attended to on certain dates, such as appointments, meetings and deadlines, have to be listed in the diary in order to prevent them from being forgotten. If a task has been completed it can be crossed out. If appointments, meetings and tasks have been captured in writing they need no longer be stored in the person's memory – freeing his mind for more productive and creative tasks;

- See to it that lists of tasks awaiting completion are kept up-to-date (on paper or electronically in a diary or an annexure to the diary). Divide these lists into long term projects, medium term projects, short term tasks and tasks requiring only a few minutes to complete; these lists have to be reviewed and renewed on a daily basis;

- The overall goal of the job or task has always to be kept in mind and the importance or urgency of all tasks is evaluated in the light of this goal. That determines the time allotted to each task;

- The overall goal of the job has to be stipulated in the job description of that particular position; if a person does not know exactly what is expected of him and how his efforts dovetail into the activities and goals of the whole organization a lot of time may be wasted on unnecessary and unproductive actions;

- It is always good to plan a day or a week in advance and allot enough time for every task that has to be completed in order to prevent unnecessary rushes;

- Urgent tasks with a deadline in the near future are completed first and the remaining time is utilized for less urgent tasks on the list of uncompleted tasks;

- Tasks with deadlines should be started in good time; tasks that are rushed because of approaching deadlines are usually performed less efficiently while expensive and valuable time may be wasted by correcting mistakes afterwards;

- Always strive for excellence rather than for perfection, since trying to attain perfection wastes valuable time (except in certain jobs where nothing but perfection is acceptable);

- It is always good to start the day with tasks that can be completed in less than two minutes, such as making a phone call, filing away a document or checking for e-mail – if a fairly large number of tasks can be completed in a relatively short time, then the majority of tasks on the list for that day can be crossed out within an hour;

- When a period of a few minutes becomes available use it to complete a small task;

- Where possible, less important tasks are to be delegated to inferiors (make sure that they are up to the task and make sure that they report back after completion of the task);

- It is important to learn to say "no" to certain requests for help, especially when this will mean that certain other important tasks cannot be completed or when this help means performing tasks outside the job description for that particular position;

- Documents must, if possible, be handled only once. If a letter or memorandum is received it should immediately lead to a plan of action to give effect to its contents and thereafter it should be filed. If it is not possible to deal with it at once, post it to the "pending" tray and keep it for later action, together with other documents, which have to lead to some sort of action;

- Divide incoming documents and messages in the "in" basket (letters, memoranda, e-mails and voice mails) into the following categories: junk, reference and actionable. If something is classified as junk, get rid of it. If something contains important information, file it in the appropriate file for future reference. If something needs to be acted upon, try and deal with it immediately or keep it in the "pending" tray;

- Where possible, all tasks should be completed in one go; interruptions cause a waste of time since it takes time to pick up the threads after a delay;
- Chase away people who only want to chat and waste your time while you are working;
- It isn't always possible to regulate interruptions such as incoming telephone calls or unexpected visits, but these should be handled in such a manner that the least possible time is lost;
- Avoid travelling as much as possible; rather use the telephone, the fax machine, text messages or e-mail to communicate with people elsewhere;
- If face-to-face meetings are essential, it is profitable to invite the other person to your office instead of travelling elsewhere;
- Records should be kept of all phone calls, interviews, conversations and meetings and these records should be kept in the appropriate files for future reference. Write down the date and time of the note because it may be important in future to know exactly when the relevant conversation or meeting took place; and
- Keep your working space tidy; throw out all pieces of junk, keep your files and books with reference material in one place, keep your files with correspondence in another place, arrange your equipment and utensils in such a manner as to minimize unnecessary movement and sort your supplies (paper, stamps, paper clips, staples, pens etcetera) into different categories and store them in drawers or trays. This will help you not to waste time while looking for a specific item.

34. MANAGING DANGERS AND CHALLENGES

Read: Acts 20: 28–32; Rev 3: 2–5 & 15–22
Describe the dangers the church face. How are these dangers to be faced?

Read: Prov 3: 5–6; Luke 14: 28–32; James 4: 13–16
Does it mean that we don't trust God if we make plans for the future?

It is necessary that a church council, or one of its committees, regularly undertake a so-called SWOT analysis. This analysis looks at the following factors affecting the future of that particular church:

- **S**trong points;
- **W**eak points;
- **O**pportunities; and
- **T**hreats.

The church cannot isolate itself from the world, but is called to serve God and humanity within this world with all its dangers, temptations, opportunities and challenges.

That means that a thorough appraisal of the environment in which the church is operating should be done. The following factors should receive attention:

- The needs of the community;
- Crime statistics;

- Social problems, such as drug abuse, domestic violence, unemployment, the suicide rate, the neglect of elderly people and teenage pregnancies;
- Health problems caused by the circumstances in which people live; and
- Challenges posed by undesirable media exposure, such as pornography and anti-Christian propaganda.

These factors will reveal which threats and challenges have to be faced. The persons conducting the analysis should also ask themselves:

- How much manpower do we have and what expertise do these people have?
- Can we rely on state departments and non-governmental organizations for assistance?
- What are our assets and financial position?
- What are our weaknesses and failures?

This part of the analysis will also show which opportunities are present and on which strengths the church can rely, as well as weaknesses that have to be overcome.

The results of this analysis should lead to a plan of action. It has already been mentioned that contingency plans ought to be drawn up to handle all sorts of emergencies. The SWOT analysis will help to draw up realistic plans.

The Army has an old saying: "If you fail to plan you plan to fail." This is also true of the church. God gave us the ability to use our imaginations and our intelligence and with those we can anticipate future tendencies, dangers, threats, opportunities and challenges – and be ready for them.

35. THE REASON FOR THE EXISTENCE OF THE CHURCH

Much attention has been given in this book to techniques and methods how the church ought to be led, managed and administered. All these actions should aid the church to stay healthy, to grow and to fulfill the reasons for her existence.

This all boils down to the fact that God founded the church with one overriding objective: the church exists in order to further the interests of the Kingdom of God. How this is to be realized in practice can, perhaps, best be illustrated when the various metaphors for the church in the New Testament are investigated. The New Testament describes the church as –

- The bride of Christ;
- The body of Christ;
- The temple of the Holy Spirit and the dwelling of God;
- The people of God;
- The army of Jesus Christ;
- The flock of Jesus Christ; and
- The household of God.

Each of these metaphors has to be described separately.

The Bride of Christ
Every wedding is a joyous occasion. The wedding of the Lamb (Jesus Christ) and his bride (the body of believers) is described in Rev 19: 7. We also read in Rev 21: 2 – "I saw the holy city, New Jerusalem, coming down out of heaven from God, made ready as a bride adorned for her husband."

When a bridegroom and a bride get married, they promise to stay faithful, to love each other and to serve each other. Jesus Christ demonstrated his love for his bride when he was crucified. He still protects his church against the attacks of Satan and prepares a heavenly feast for Judgment Day and his second coming, when this marriage will be celebrated and consummated in the heavenly New Jerusalem.

Paul saw the relationship between husband and wife as a parallel with the relationship between Christ and his church (Eph 5: 22–32).

Each one of us has to ask himself: is my church loyal to Jesus Christ? Are all our actions and programs aimed at demonstrating our love for Him? Are we keeping ourselves pure from contamination by the sins of this world?

The Body of Christ
This metaphor is mentioned in 1 Cor 12: 18–24; Eph 4: 12 and Col 1: 18. Christians are supposed to be the eyes, ears, feet, hands, mouth and heart of Jesus. Just as a human body forms a unity where all parts work seamlessly together, so the church of Christ ought to be a unity – on local level, but also world-wide.

Unfortunately, this unity is not always visible. There is often disunity, strife, jealousy and competition between different churches and between Christians, instead of co-operation, mutual love and mutual support.

We are supposed to continue the work that Jesus started when He was alive on earth – feeding the hungry, visiting the sick, helping the downtrodden, defending the defenseless and proclaiming God's kingship over his whole creation.

The Temple of the Holy Spirit and the Dwelling of God
There were many temples in the time of the Bible. The Jews worshipped at the temple in Jerusalem, while pagans worshipped their gods in a multitude of temples in many countries. It was thought that God, as well as these pagan deities, resided in their temples, although they also had their dwellings somewhere in the sky or in heaven.

God, the Father of Jesus Christ, whom we as Christians worship as the only God, doesn't have an earthly temple built of stone or other materials. The temple in Jerusalem became superfluous after the time of Jesus and, therefore, God allowed it to be destroyed by the Roman army in AD 70. His primary dwelling is in heaven, but He also resides within the church (1 Cor 3: 9).

Paul writes in Eph 2: 20–22 that the body of believers amounts to a building, "being built on the foundation of the apostles and prophets, Christ Jesus himself being the chief cornerstone; in whom the whole building, fitted together, grows into a holy temple in the Lord; in whom you also are built together for a habitation of God in the Spirit."

This leads to the question: is my local church a fitting abode for God? Does He feel at home in our congregation? Are all our actions designed in such a manner than outsiders can see that our church is a temple of the Holy Spirit?

The People of God

The people of Israel were God's people in the time of the Old Testament. That changed after the time when Jesus Christ was on earth. We read in 1 Pet 2: 9–10 –

> "But you are an elect race, a royal priesthood, a holy nation, a people for God's own possession, that you may show forth the excellencies of him who called you out of darkness into his marvelous light: who in time past were no people, but now are the people of God, who had not obtained mercy, but now have obtained mercy."

These words were written to people who were not born as Jews but came from a pagan background before they converted to Christianity. In the same vein, all believers in our time can be seen as the people of God. Our king is Jesus Christ and we are his subjects. We ought to obey his laws of love, charity, compassion, tolerance, forgiveness and justice because our first loyalty is with Him.

The Army of Jesus Christ

Paul reminded his readers in 2 Tim 2: 3–4 –

> "You therefore must endure hardship, as a good soldier of Christ Jesus. No soldier on service entangles himself in the affairs of life, that he may please him who enrolled him as a soldier."

Soldiers are trained to fight a war. Our war is against Satan and his works – injustice, immorality, dishonesty, corruption, hate, ignorance and jealousy. Any army can only win a war if the soldiers are disciplined, efficiently organized and well trained. They have to obey the orders of their superiors. Our general is none other than Jesus Christ who is the perfect leader and commander-in-chief and we have the promise in many places in Scripture that his battle against the forces of darkness will end in total victory. In Eph 6: 11-18 we find a description of the weapons of a soldier of Jesus Christ.

Jesus demonstrated his superiority over Satan by being resurrected after his crucifixion and his elevation into heavenly glory. We may share in his victory.

The Flock of Jesus Christ

Jesus calls Himself "the Good Shepherd" (John 10: 11). A shepherd has the task of looking after his flock, keeping the sheep out of danger and feeding them. That is what Jesus Christ does to his flock, the body of believers. We may, therefore, rely on Him and follow Him wherever He leads us.

The pastors and elders of a congregation are also shepherds (Acts 20: 28; 1 Pet 5: 2) and it is expected that they follow the example of the Good Shepherd by guiding the flock correctly and with care.

The Household of God

Christians are the children of God (John 1: 12). For that reason, Paul addressed his fellow-believers as "brothers" and "sisters". We all have the same heavenly Father and we constitute the household of God (Eph 2: 19). Our eldest brother is the Son of God, Jesus Christ. It is expected of members of a household to love each other, support each other and defend each other. Is that true of the church to which we belong?

Members of the same household like to be in each other's company. Do we have the habit of visiting the house of God where we can worship our heavenly Father every Sunday, together with our brothers and sisters in Jesus Christ?

Conclusion

Only one conclusion can be drawn from all this: the church does not exist for its own sake. Its only reason to exist is to serve. It has to serve the interests of the Kingdom of God and that means that it has to –

- Proclaim the Gospel;
- Worship God;
- Educate adults and children on how to become better servants of God;
- Support those who suffer poverty, pain, injustice, loneliness and bereavement;
- Be a positive force in the community;
- Fight injustice, crime, strife, hatred and corruption; and
- Promote justice, the rule of law, peace and compassion.

These goals can only be reached if the church is led, managed and administered effectively and efficiently according to biblical principles. It is, therefore, not a luxury to spend time on better administrative and management systems; these systems are essential for the church to be true to its calling.

BIBLIOGRAPHY

Translation of the Bible
Passages from the Bible are quoted from the *World English Bible* as found on a CD with the title *The Bible Collection, Deluxe Edition*, and published by ValuSoft, a division of THQ Inc, Waconia MN, 2002.
The above-mentioned CD also contains the Greek text of the New Testament, as well as *Strong's Complete Greek & Hebrew Lexicon*.

Literature
Note: The following publications were consulted while writing this book, although not all of them are mentioned in footnotes:

Adair, J.   *Effective Teambuilding.*   London: Pan, 1986.
————— . *Effective Motivation : how to get Extraordinary Results from Everyone.*   London: Pan, 1996.
Allen, D.   *Getting Things Done : the Art of Stress-free Productivity.*   London: Piatkus, 2008.
Anstey, M.   *Negotiating Conflict :   Insights and Skills for Negotiators and Peacemakers.*   Cape Town: Juta & Co, 1991.
Ardrey, Robert. *The Territorial Imperative : a Personal Inquiry into the Animal Origins of Property and Nations.*   London: Collins, 1970.
Brekke, M.L. et al.   *Ten Faces of Ministry: Perspectives on Pastoral and Congregational Effectiveness Based on a Survey of 5000 Lutherans.* Minneapolis: Augsburg, 1979.
Coens, T. and N. Jenkins. *Abolishing Performance Appraisals: why they Backfire and what to Do Instead.*   San Francisco: Berrett-Koehler P, 2002.
Food, P. and C. Gibson. *Management and Employment: the*

Recruitment, Development and Motivation of People.
Kenilworth: Ampersand, 2002.

Frankl, Viktor Emil. *The Will to Meaning: Foundations and Applications of Logotherapy.* *S.l.*: Meridian, 1988.

Gellerman, S.W. *Motivation in the Real World: the Art of Getting Extra Effort from Everyone – Including Yourself.* New York: Dutton, 1992.

Hall, D.T. "The Effect of the Individual on an Organization's Structure, Style, and Process." In *Performance Measurement and Theory,* edited by F. Landy. Hillsdale, N.J.: Lawrence Erlbaum, 1983.

Hendrix, O. *Management for Christian Leaders.* Grand Rapids: Baker, 1992.

Heyns, L.M and H.J.C. Pieterse. *Eerste Treë in die Praktiese Teologie.* Pretoria: Gnosis, 1990.

Hilliard, V.G. *Performance Improvement in the Public Sector.* Pretoria: Van Schaik, 1995.

Johnson, J.J. *Die Kerklike Beheer van Stoflike Aangeleenthede : 'n Kerkregtelike Evaluering van Artikel 57 van die Kerkorde van die Nederduitse Gereformeerde Kerk.* Stellenbosch: Stellenbosch University (D.Th. thesis), 1994.

Lennick, D. and F. Kiel. *Moral Intelligence: Enhancing Business Performance and Leadership Success.* Upper Saddle River, NJ: Wharton School Publishing. 2008.

Louw, Daniel. *Pastoraal en Ontmoeting: Ontwerp vir 'n Basisteorie, Antropologie, Metode en Terapie.* Pretoria: RGN, 1993.

Margrave, A. and R. Gordon. *The Complete Idiot's Guide to Performance Appraisals.* Alpha, 2001.

Martens, J.T. *Die Rol van die Predikant in die Gemeente: 'n*

Sosiologiese Teoretiese Model. Stellenbosch: Universiteit van Stellenbosch (Lic.Theol. thesis), 1978.

M^CConnon, S and M. M^CConnon. *Resolving Conflict: Establish Trusting and Productive Relationships in the Workplace.* Oxford: How To Books, 2002.

Meadow, Mary Jo and Richard D. Kahoe, *Psychology of Religion.* New York: Harper & Row, 1984.

Meares, L.B. "A Model for Changing Organizational Culture." *Personnel:* 38–42, July 1986.

Miller, R.F. *Running a Meeting that Works.* London: Cassell, 1995.

Mulholland, J. *The Language of Negotiation: A Handbook of Practical Strategies in Improving Communication.* London: Routledge, 1991.

Pattison, E.M. *Pastor and Parish: A Systems Approach.* Philadelphia: Fortress, 1977.

Rossouw, H.W. *Die Sin van die Lewe.* Kaapstad: Tafelberg, 1981.

Schein, E.H. *Organizational Psychology.* Englewood Cliffs: Prentice-Hall, 1988.

Scholtz, David Adelbert. *Die Amp en die Vrou in die Kerk.* Stellenbosch: Stellenbosch University (M.Th. Thesis), 1988.[32]

————. *Die Voorspelling van Beroepsukses Onder 'n Groep Diensdoende Predikante.* Potchefstroom: Potchefstroom University for Higher Christian Education (Ph.D. Dissertation), 1997.[33]

Shermer, M. *The Believing Brain : from Ghosts and Gods and*

---

[32] Translation of title: *The Offices and Women in the Church.*

[33] Translation of title: *The Prediction of Occupational Success Amongst a Group of Serving Ministers.*

Conspiracies – how we Construct Beliefs and Reinforce them as Truths. New York: St Martin's, 2011.
Tosi, H.L. et al. *Managing Organizational Behavior*. New York : Harper Collins, 1990.
Van Schoor, M. *What is Communication?* Pretoria: J.L. Van Schaik, 1986.

Picture Credits
Outside Cover
Jesus washing the feet of his disciples, Monastery of Hosios Loukas, Greece
https://daydreamtourist.com/2013/11/13/hosios-loukas/

Frontispiece
Albrecht Dürer – The Last Supper (1523)
https://commons.wikimedia.org/wiki/File:Albrecht_D%C3%BCrer_-_The_Last_Supper_-_WGA7259.jpg